English Password

A complete course for GCSE

August
1988.

John Griffin
Theresa Sullivan

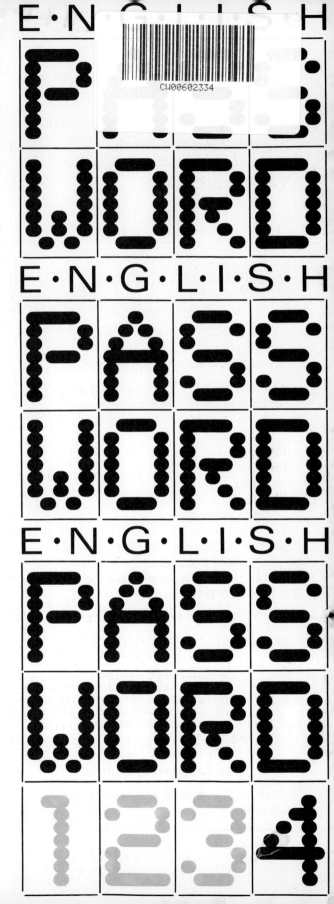

Contents

1 Whose responsibility?   11

Speak out!

2 The language of selling   35

4

Introducing the book

Each section has three parts:

1 Extracts for study

The passages in this book represent the many different purposes and styles of writing such as

— prose – fiction and non-fiction
— poems
— plays
— newspaper reports
— transcripts of speech
— advertisements
— diaries

You will be asked to show you have understood

— the content and purpose of each passage
— how its style suits its purpose

by answering questions on

— the facts and
— the inferences (the meaning which lies below the surface)

You will be asked to

— reorganise and redraft the material
— summarise and select
— imitate the style and method

Passages will lead to discussion in pairs, small groups or as a whole class, sometimes in role
and to various forms of direct writing, including

— narrative
— descriptive
— presenting a point of view
— reflective

and various types of practical assignments such as

— letters
— reports
— surveys

In each case you will be asked to show

- a sense of the audience for whom you are writing
- an awareness of the appropriate style

2 Language practice

This looks in closer details at the importance of *style* and *accuracy*. You will be asked to

- study and comment on pieces written by students of your own age
- take a close look at the language of newspapers, the law, selling
- widen your vocabulary
- improve and extend your own sentence construction
- consider what distinguishes speech from written language

3 Examination practice

All the sections end with examination-type questions for you to attempt. These questions cover a wide range of the types of questions you will meet in the examination, including

- showing your understanding of the author's purpose, and the ways he or she has tried to achieve it
- responding to a passage from a novel, a poem or a play by writing of your own
- writing a letter or a report
- filling in a form
- giving your views
- summarising
- writing an account
- demonstrating your ability to write accurately and appropriately

Skills reference section

At the end of the book you will find a Skills reference section, which you can use to check points of punctuation or spelling when you feel unsure.

Other skills where you might need more help are included in the various chapters.

The examination

The new GCSE examinations in English and English Literature must fulfil the requirements of the National Criteria, which are guidelines drawn up on behalf of the government.

When you have completed this book, you will have had the opportunity to practise all aspects of the National Criteria for English and English Literature.

Those for English require you to be able to

1 **understand** and **convey** information
2 **understand**, **order** and **present** facts, ideas and opinions
3 **evaluate** (judge) information in reading material and in other media (other forms of writing), and **select** what is relevant to specific purposes
4 **articulate** (put into words) experience and **express** what you feel and what you imagine
5 **recognise** implicit meaning and attitudes (i.e. what is implied)
6 show a **sense of audience** and an awareness of **style** in both **formal** and **informal** situations
7 exercise control of **appropriate grammatical structures**, conventions of **paragraphing**, **sentence structure**, **punctuation** and **spelling** in your writing
8 **communicate** effectively and appropriately in your spoken English

The criteria for English Literature require you to be able to

1 understand literary texts in ways which may range from a grasp of their **surface meaning** to a **deeper awareness** of their **themes** and **attitudes**
2 recognise and appreciate ways in which writers **use** language
3 recognise and appreciate other ways in which writers achieve their effects (e.g. **structure**, **characterisation**)
4 communicate a **sensitive** and **informed** response to what you read

1 Whose responsibility?

Speak out!

The theme of this section is the courage needed to speak out against injustice that does not directly involve you.

You are asked to

──────→ Examine, interpret and judge a poem

──────→ Discuss the poem's wider meaning

──────→ Explore the meaning through improvisation

──────→ Examine, interpret and judge a prose passage

──────→ Compare and contrast prose and poetry treatments of the same theme

──────→ Describe a similar occasion from your own experience

──────→ Criticise a student's writing on the subject

Examination practice – answer questions on a short story

A POEM AND A NOVEL COMPARED

The Hangman

1   Into our town the Hangman came,
    Smelling of gold and blood and fame –
    And he paced our streets with a sinister air
    And built his frame on the courthouse square.

5   The scaffold stood by the courthouse side,
    Only as wide as the door was wide;
    A frame as tall, or little more,
    Than the capping sill of the courthouse door.

    And we wondered, whenever we had the time,
10   Who was the criminal, what the crime
    As the Hangman prepared with an expert twist
    The yellow rope in his busy fist.

    And guiltless though we were, with dread
    We passed his eyes like buckshot lead;
15   Till one of us cried, 'Hangman! Who is he
    For whom you raise the gallows-tree?'

    Then a twinkle grew in the buckshot eye
    And he gave us a riddle in way of reply:
    'He who serves me best,' said he,
20   'Shall hang by the rope on the gallows-tree.'

    And he stepped down, and laid his hand
    On a man who came from a foreign land –
    And we breathed again; for another's grief
    At the Hangman's hand brought us relief.

25   And the gallows-frame on the courthouse lawn
    By tomorrow would be pulled down and gone.
    So we gave him way, and no one spoke
    Out of respect for his Hangman's cloak.

    The next day's sun looked mildly down
30   On roof and street in our quiet town
    And, stark and black in the morning air
    Stood the gallows still on the courthouse square.

    And the Hangman stood at his usual stand,
    With the yellow rope in his busy hand;
35   With his buckshot eye and his jaw like a pike
    And his air so knowing and businesslike.

And we cried, 'Hangman, have you not done
Yesterday, with the foreign one?'
Then he stood still and said, amazed:
40 'Oh, not for him was the gallows raised . . .'

He laughed a laugh as he looked at us:
'. . . Did you think I'd gone to all this fuss
To hang one man? That's a thing I do
Just to stretch the rope when it is new.'

45 Then one of us dared to shout out 'Shame!'
And into our midst the Hangman came
To that man's place. 'So you will side,' said he,
'With him that was meat for the gallows-tree?'

And he laid his hand on that man's arm,
50 And we shrank back in quick alarm,
And we gave him way, and no one spoke
Out of the fear for his Hangman's cloak.

That night we saw with dread surprise
The Hangman's scaffold had grown in size.
55 Fed by the blood beneath the chute
The gallows-tree had taken root;

It was now as wide, and a little more,
Than the steps which led to the courthouse door,
And tall as the writing, or nearly as tall,
60 Halfway up on the courthouse wall.

The third he took – (we had all heard tell) –
Was a traitor and an infidel.
'I hope,' said the Hangman, 'you've nothing to say
In defence of this Jew who's to hang today?'

65 And we cried out, 'Is this one he
Who has served you well and faithfully?'
'Not he,' said the Hangman. 'I just needed a man
To check my new gallows was built to plan.'

The next he chose for the scaffold's climb
70 Was old and sick, well past his prime.
The Hangman said, 'Will anyone try
To save a wretch so near to die?'

The fifth. The sixth. And we cried again:
'Hangman! Hangman, is this the man?'
75 'Not yet,' he said. 'We all shall know
When the man who served me best must go.'

And so we ceased and asked no more,
As the Hangman tallied his bloody score;

And sun by sun, and night by night,
80 The gallows grew to monstrous height.

The wings of the scaffold opened wide
Till they covered the square from side to side;
And the monster cross-beam, looking down,
Cast its shadow across the town.

85 Then through the town the Hangman came
And called in the empty streets, my name –
And I looked at the gallows soaring tall
And thought, 'There's no-one left at all

For hanging; and so he calls to me
90 To help pull down the gallows-tree.'
And I went out with right good hope
To the Hangman's tree and the Hangman's rope.

He smiled at me as I came down
To the courthouse square through the silent town,
95 And supple and stretched in his busy hand
Was the yellow twist of the hempen strand

And he whistled his tune as he tried the trap
And it sprang down with a ready snap –
And then with a smile of awful command
100 He laid his hand upon my hand.

'You tricked me, Hangman!' I shouted then,
'That your scaffold was built for other men . . .
I've never served you at all,' I cried,
'You lied to me, Hangman, foully lied.'

105 Then a twinkle grew in the buckshot eye:
'Lied to you? Tricked you?' he said, 'Not I.
For I answered straight and I told you true:
The scaffold was raised for none but YOU.

For who has served more faithfully
110 Than you with your coward's hope?' said he,
'And where are the others who might have stood
Side by your side in the common good?'

'Dead,' I whispered; and bowed my knee.
'Murdered,' the Hangman corrected me;
115 'First the foreigner, then the Jew . . .
I did no more than you let me do.'

Benéath the béam that blócked the ský
Nóne had stóod so alóne as Í –
And the Hángman strápped me, and nó vóice thére
120 Cried, 'Stáy!' for mé in the émpty squáre.

Maurice Ogden

14

A note on the Understanding sections in this book

Most passages are followed by an Understanding section; the questions can either be answered in writing or they can be a basis for class discussion. Their aim is to help your appreciation and enjoyment of the passage, so that you will feel more confident in tackling the oral and written assignments based on the passage.

Understanding the poem

The Hangman is a narrative poem; it tells a story in verse.

Decide which of these is the main purpose of the poem.

1 To tell a story of cruelty and injustice.
2 To make a point about one of the worst aspects of human nature.
3 To combat racial prejudice.
4 To illustrate the cruelty of some systems of government.

The poet could have made his point in one sentence. By choosing a narrative poem he is hoping to make his point dramatic and memorable.

How the poet makes his point memorable

1 Pick out the details in the first four verses which contribute to making the Hangman a dreaded figure.
2 'Whenever we had the time.' What does this phrase suggest about the townspeople's interest in the Hangman when he first arrives?
3 What are the townspeople's feelings about the first two hangings? About the later hangings?
4 The Hangman's scaffold had grown in size.
  Fed by the blood beneath the chute
  The gallows-tree had taken root.
This cannot be literally true. In what way has the gallows grown because of the blood spilt? What other parts of the poem are not literally true? What is their purpose?
5 The Hangman said at the beginning that the hanging was for 'He who serves me best'. In what sense is the narrator the one who served him best?
6 ' "Dead," I whispered.' Why do you think the narrator whispers?
7 Why is it fitting that there is no one to cry 'Stay!' for the narrator?

The importance of rhythm

The syllables marked ´ in the last verse are the ones emphasised by the rhythm; the words emphasised are the important ones in the verse. Which ones are most important to stress? Why?

Words at the beginning and end of lines stand out. Which important words are emphasised in this way?

The second word of a rhymed pair is particularly emphasised. Which words has this stressed? Why are they particularly important?

How has the poet altered the natural word order of the second line to further stress *I*?

Choose two other verses and write briefly about the way rhyme and rhythm have stressed important words.

Discussion

> **So we gave him way, and no one spoke**
> **Out of respect for his Hangman's cloak.**

The Hangman's cloak is his *uniform.* The cloak identifies his job and gives him authority.

Name three or four other uniforms that we take notice of and respect. Do people who wear uniforms as part of their job have authority when they are in their ordinary clothes? Would we still respect their jobs if uniform was abolished? In what ways can a person abuse the fact that he or she wears a uniform? Should teachers wear a uniform?

> **First the foreigner, then the Jew.**

The crowd breathed a sigh of relief when the Hangman chose the foreigner. Why is this easier for them to accept than if he had chosen one of them straight away? Why do we need to make a great effort to accept a foreigner? Do we treat as foreign those who come from another country? Or those from another school? Town/village? Street?

Do you agree with the statement: 'When we go abroad, we don't meet foreigners; we are the foreigners'?

> **'I did no more than you let me do.'**

The Hangman says that the responsibility for the hangings lies not with him but with the narrator. Where do you think the responsibility lies? How far do you think a politician for whom people have voted is justified in saying 'I did no more than you let me do'?

Role-play

Parts

the Hangman
the narrator
the person who cried 'Shame!'
the crowd of townspeople
reader(s) – the person telling the story will need to be involved in the action

It would perhaps be best if the verses were split up between the whole group, so that everybody has a chance to read.

Props

a rope
a cloak
if possible, a platform with steps leading up to it

You will need to find some way of representing the hanging. Try out different ways to find which is the most effective.

You will need to consider:

> how to make the Hangman a frightening figure
> how the townspeople react when he comes into town
> how they react to each of the hangings
> how to make it clear that the gallows is growing larger

Improvisation 1

When you have become familiar with what happens in the poem, improvise the story without using the scripts.

Improvisation 2

In pairs hold these interviews.

1 A is the last person in the town. The Hangman has not yet called him/her. B is a newspaper reporter who has heard rumours about what has been happening in the town and has come to question A.

2 B is the Hangman. A is the reporter who, after the last person has been hanged, comes to question B.

Each partner should spend about ten minutes separately in preparation: the reporter to think of questions to ask, and the last person alive or the Hangman to prepare a story which builds upon the poem. For example, decide who is the last person living. How old is he/she? What does he/she do for a living? What has happened to his/her family?

Writing

1 Write up the results of your interview as a newspaper article. Think of a striking headline for your article.
2 Write a story with a moral illustrating what seems to you to be an important human failing. Think about your audience. Make it a children's story if you wish.

Looking at poetry

Poetry is simply another medium for expressing a feeling, an idea or a point of view, like prose or drama, or television or radio. A poem's value, therefore, lies in its meaning, not in its form, its rhythm or rhyme. These help to communicate feelings or thoughts more clearly, but they have no value in themselves.

   Although everyone can immediately recognise the difference between poetry and prose, there are many different forms of poetry. Look at these.

a) **Mushrooms**   Sylvia Plath

   Overnight, very
   Whitely, discreetly
   Very quietly.

b) **Self-pity**   D H Lawrence

   I never saw a wild thing
   sorry for itself
   A small bird will drop frozen dead from a bough
   without ever having felt sorry for itself

c) **The Darlaston Dog Fight**   Tom Langley

   Down Sewerage Street where the smell ain't so sweet
   Rough Mog flopped down on his flat-bottomed feet
   And under his arm The Pride of 'Em All
   The bitch as could bite a bolt hole through a wall

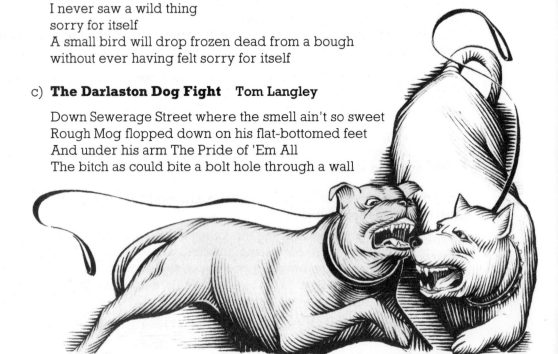

d) **Girl, Boy, Flower, Bicycle**   N K Joseph

This girl
Waits at the corner for
This boy
Freewheeling on his bicycle

e) **A Negro Woman**   William Carlos Williams

carrying a bunch of marigolds
wrapped
in an old newspaper

f) **The Politician's Epitaph**   poet unknown

Here richly with ridiculous display
The politician's corpse is laid away
While all of his acquaintance sneered and slanged
I wept, for I had longed to see him hanged.

Write a prose version of each to discover what advantage the poet has gained from the form of writing chosen. Notice how the form of the verse suits the poem's purpose: whether descriptive, making a point, making a story, or humorous.

Certain words or phrases may be isolated and therefore emphasised by the verse form. These will probably be words important to the poet's meaning. Notice how *sorry for itself* is emphasised in (b). Words at the ends of lines are stressed, particularly rhymed ones. *Hanged* in (f) is the climax of the poem, giving the reader a shock after *wept.*

The rushing primitive rhythm of (c) is suitable to a narrative poem, while the slower rhythms of (b) and (e) are suitable for reflection and description.

Choose one of these formats and use it to try to make a point, convey a feeling or describe a person or place. You will find (b), (d) and (e) are the easiest to imitate. Do not strive for rhyme, or you will sacrifice sense.

Your own poem

Using the form of *one* of the poems above as a model write a poem (about ten lines) on one of these subjects:

1 a description of a person whose appearance you find striking in some way.
2 a protest about some regulation or system that you think is unnecessarily restrictive.
3 a reflection about a particular time of the year (Christmas or spring, for example).
4 a humorous piece about a day when you could not seem to do anything right.

Brother Leon

*Here is a passage from a novel which makes the
same point as the poem. It is set in a private
Catholic boys' school in America.*

1 Brother Leon was getting ready to put on his show. Jerry knew the symptoms –
all the guys knew them. Most of them were freshmen and had been in Leon's
class only a month or so but the teacher's pattern had already emerged. First,
Leon gave them a reading assignment. Then he'd pace up and down, up and
5 down, restless, sighing, wandering through the aisles, the blackboard pointer
poised in his hand, the pointer he used either like a conductor's baton or a
musketeer's sword. He'd use the tip to push around a book on a desk or to
flick a kid's necktie, scratching gently down some guy's back, poking the
pointer as if he were a rubbish collector picking his way through the debris of
10 the classroom. One day, the pointer had rested on Jerry's head for a moment,
and then passed on. Unaccountably, Jerry had shivered, as if he had just
escaped some terrible fate.

  Now, aware of Leon prowling ceaseless around the classroom, Jerry kept
his eyes on the paper although he didn't feel like reading. Two more periods.
15 He looked forward to football practice. After days of exercises, the coach had
said that probably he'd let them use the ball this afternoon.
  'Enough of this crap.'
  That was Brother Leon – always trying to shock. Using words like crap and
bull and slipping in a few damns and hells once in a while. Actually, he did
20 shock. Maybe because the words were so startling as they issued from this
pale and inoffensive-looking little man. Later on, you found out that he wasn't
inoffensive, of course. Now, everyone looked up at Leon as that word crap

echoed in the room. Ten minutes left – time enough for Leon to perform, to play one of his games. The class looked at him in a kind of horrible fascination.

25   The Brother's glance went slowly around the room, like the ray of a lighthouse sweeping a familiar coast, searching for hidden defects. Jerry felt a sense of dread and anticipation, both at the same time.
'Bailey,' Leon said.
'Yes, Brother Leon.' Leon *would* pick Bailey: one of the weak kids, high
30   honour student, but shy, introverted, always reading, his eyes red-rimmed behind the glasses.
'Up here,' Leon said, finger beckoning.
Bailey went quietly to the front of the room. Jerry could see a vein throbbing in the boy's temple.
35   'As you know, gentlemen,' Brother Leon began, addressing the class directly and ignoring Bailey completely although the boy was standing beside him, 'as you know, a certain discipline must be maintained in a school. A line must be drawn between teachers and students. We teachers would love to be one of the boys, of course. But that line of separation must remain. An invisible
40   line, perhaps, but still there.' His moist eyes gleamed. 'After all, you can't see the wind but it's there. You see its handiwork, bending the trees, stirring the leaves . . .'
As he spoke, he gestured, his arm becoming the wind, the pointer in his hand following the direction of the wind and suddenly, without warning,
45   striking Bailey on the cheek. The boy leaped backwards in pain and surprise.
'Bailey, I'm sorry,' Leon said, but his voice lacked apology. Had it been an accident? Or another of Leon's little cruelties?

Now all eyes were on the stricken Bailey. Brother Leon studied him, looking at him as if he were a specimen under a microscope, as if the specimen
50   contained the germ of some deadly disease. You had to hand it to Leon – he was a superb actor. He loved to read short stories aloud, taking all the parts, providing all the sound effects. Nobody yawned or fell asleep in Leon's class. You had to be alert every minute, just as everyone was alert now, looking at Bailey, wondering what Leon's next move would be. Under Leon's steady
55   gaze, Bailey had stopped stroking his cheek, even though a pink welt had appeared, like an evil stain spreading on his flesh. Somehow, the tables were turned. Now it seemed as if Bailey had been at fault all along, that Bailey had committed an error, had stood in the wrong place at the wrong time and had caused his own misfortune. Jerry squirmed in his chair. Leon gave him the
60   creeps, the way he could change the atmosphere in a room without even speaking a word.

'Bailey,' Leon said. But not looking at Bailey, looking at the class as if they were all in on a joke that Bailey knew nothing about. As if the class and Leon were banded together in a secret conspiracy.
65   'Yes, Brother Leon?' Bailey asked, his eyes magnified behind the glasses.
A pause.

'Bailey,' Brother Leon said. 'Why do you find it necessary to cheat?'

They say the hydrogen bomb makes no noise: there's only a blinding white flash that strikes cities dead. The noise comes after the flash, after the silence.
70 That's the kind of silence that blazed in the classroom now.

Bailey stood speechless, his mouth an open wound.

'Is silence an admission of guilt, Bailey?' Brother Leon asked, turning to the boy at last.

Bailey shook his head frantically. Jerry felt his own head shaking,
75 joining Bailey in silent denial.

'Ah, Bailey,' Leon sighed, his voice fluttering with sadness. 'What are we going to do about you?' Turning towards the class again, buddies with them – him and the class against the cheat.

'I don't cheat, Brother Leon,' Bailey said, his voice a kind of squeak.
80 'But look at the evidence, Bailey. Your marks – all *A*'s, no less. Every test, every paper, every homework assignment. Only a genius is capable of that sort of performance. Do you claim to be a genius, Bailey?' Toying with him. 'I'll admit you look like one – those glasses, that pointed chin, that wild hair . . .'

85 Leon leaned towards the class, tossing his own chin, awaiting the approval of laughter, everything in his manner suggesting the response of laughter from the class. And it came. They laughed. Hey, what's going on here, Jerry wondered even as he laughed with them. Because Bailey did somehow look like a genius or at least a caricature of the mad scientist in old movies.
90 'Bailey,' Brother Leon said, turning his full attention to the boy again as the laughter subsided.

'Yes,' Bailey replied miserably.

'You haven't answered my question.' He walked deliberately to the window and was suddenly absorbed in the street outside, the September leaves
95 turning brown and crisp.

Bailey stood alone at the front of the class, as if he was facing a firing squad. Jerry felt his cheeks getting warm, throbbing with the warmth.

'Well, Bailey?' From Leon at the window, still intent on the world outside.

'I don't cheat, Brother Leon,' Bailey said, a surge of strength in his voice,
100 like he was taking a last stand.

'Then how do you account for all those *A*'s?'

'I don't know.'

Brother Leon whirled around. 'Are you perfect, Bailey? All those *A*'s – that implies perfection. Is that the answer, Bailey?'
105 For the first time, Bailey looked at the class itself, in silent appeal, like something wounded, lost, abandoned.

'Only God is perfect, Bailey.'

Jerry's neck began to hurt. And his lungs burned. He realised he'd been holding his breath. He gulped air, carefully, not wanting to move a muscle. He
110 wished he was invisible. He wished he wasn't here in the classroom. He wanted to be out on the football field, fading back, looking for a receiver.

'Do you compare yourself with God, Bailey?'

Cut it out, Brother, cut it out, Jerry cried silently.

'If God is perfect and you are perfect, Bailey, does that suggest something to
115 you?'

Bailey didn't answer, eyes wide in disbelief. The class was utterly silent.
Jerry could hear the hum of the electric clock – he'd never realised before that
electric clocks hummed.

'The other alternative, Bailey, is that you are not perfect. And, of course,
120 you're not.' Leon's voice softened. 'I know you wouldn't consider anything so
sacrilegious.'

'That's right, Brother Leon,' Bailey said, relieved.

'Which leaves us with only one conclusion,' Leon said, his voice bright and
triumphant, as if he had made an important discovery. 'You cheat!'
125 In that moment, Jerry hated Brother Leon. He could taste the hate in his
stomach – it was acid, foul, burning.

'You're a cheat, Bailey. And a liar.' The words like whips.

You rat, Jerry thought. You bastard.

A voice boomed from the rear of the classroom. 'Aw, let the kid alone.'
130 Leon whipped around. 'Who said that?' His moist eyes glistened.

The bell rang, ending the period. Feet scuffled as the boys pushed back
their chairs, preparing to leave, to get out of that terrible place.

'Wait a minute,' Brother Leon said. Softly – but heard by everyone. 'Nobody
moves.'
135 The students settled in their chairs again.

Brother Leon regarded them pityingly, shaking his head, a sad and dismal
smile on his lips. 'You poor fools,' he said. 'You idiots. Do you know who's the
best one here? The bravest of all?' He placed his hand on Bailey's shoulder.
'Gregory Bailey, that's who. He denied cheating. He stood up to my
140 accusations. He stood his ground! But you, gentlemen, you sat there and
enjoyed yourselves. And those of you who didn't enjoy yourselves allowed it
to happen, allowed me to proceed. You turned this classroom into Nazi
Germany for a few moments. Yes, yes, someone finally protested. *Aw, let the
kid alone.*' Mimicking the deep voice perfectly. 'A feeble protest, too little and
145 too late.' There was scuffling in the corridors, students waiting to enter. Leon
ignored the noise. He turned to Bailey, touched the top of his head with the
pointer as if he were bestowing knighthood. 'You did well, Bailey. I'm proud
of you. You passed the biggest test of all – you were true to yourself.' Bailey's
chin was wobbling all over the place. 'Of course you don't cheat, Bailey,' his
150 voice tender and paternal. He gestured towards the class – he was a great one
for gestures. 'Your classmates out there. They're the cheaters. They cheated
you today. They're the ones who doubted you – I never did.'

Leon went to his desk. 'Dismissed,' he said, his voice filled with contempt
for all of them.

The Chocolate War by Robert Cormier

23

Understanding the passage – the elements of the story

Brother Leon

Here are groups of quotations from the passage. Say what point each group illustrates about Brother Leon. Add another quotation to each group.

1 Brother Leon was getting ready to put on his show.
  the teacher's pattern
  time enough for Leon to perform, to play one of his games.

2 he'd pace up and down, up and down,
  One day, the pointer had rested on Jerry's head for a moment, and then passed on.

3 Leon *would* pick Bailey
  Had it been an accident? Or another of Leon's little cruelties?

4 The Brother's glance went slowly around the room, like the ray of a lighthouse sweeping a familiar coast, searching for hidden defects.
  Brother Leon studied him

5 Unaccountably, Jerry had shivered
  The class looked at him in a kind of horrible fascination.
  wondering what Leon's next move would be.

6 But not looking at Bailey, looking at the class as if they were all in on a joke that Bailey knew nothing about.
  buddies with them – him and the class against the cheat.

Bailey the victim

1 Why is Bailey a suitable victim for Leon?
2 List the stages of the argument by which Brother Leon traps Bailey. The argument sounds convincing. Where is it false?

Through the eyes of Jerry

1 Brother Leon contrasts Bailey with the rest of the class:
  'But you, gentlemen, you sat there and enjoyed yourselves.'
    Decide whether Jerry's response is one of horror, enjoyment or a mixture of both. Support your answer with quotations illustrating Jerry's reactions.
2 Why do you think Jerry does not protest about the way Bailey is being treated?

Creating tension

Brother Leon treats the classroom as a stage on which he performs. He plans every move for theatrical effect. Imagine you are a director giving Brother Leon his movements. Write down his movements as a series of instructions. Here are the first four:

1 Pace up and down the aisles.
2 Use the tip of the blackboard pointer to push books, flick ties, scratch backs, and so on.
3 Glance slowly round the room.
4 Beckon Bailey to the front of the class.

Continue as far as Brother Leon walking to the window and being absorbed in the street.

The significance of the passage

1 What, at the end, does Brother Leon say is his purpose in picking on Bailey?
2 What evidence is there about Brother Leon that suggests this is not his only purpose?
3 Do you think he is justified in making his point in this way?
4 What similarities do you find between this passage and the poem, *The Hangman*?

Prose and poem – different treatments

The passage and the poem share the same theme, but treat it very differently. Make a list of the differences. Consider these elements: characterisation, use of names, setting, realism, effect of rhyme and rhythm, length, place of author in relation to story.

Discussion

Do you think Brother Leon is an exaggerated character, or could he exist? Whether he is justified or not, do you think his point is a valid one? What stops people from protesting about bullying or injustice? Are people to blame if they do not protest? What is your responsibility if you see someone being bullied?

Writing

Writing 1

Refer to your notes on how Brother Leon created tension. Write an account of a different situation in which the creation of tension is an important element.

Writing 2

Write a piece, from your own experience, about bullying. There are many types of bullying for you to choose from. You may not have been involved in physical bullying, or even bullying of the type practised by Brother Leon. You most probably have been involved in the type of bullying sometimes referred to as 'emotional blackmail', where one person sets out to make another feel guilty or embarrassed. This is the type of situation that often occurs when somebody is trying to break off a long-standing relationship, or where one member of a family conducts an emotional campaign against another. Before you begin, read and assess the sample essay on the next page; it will remind you of the points you must take into consideration for your own piece.

Writing 3

Write a piece about the causes of bullying and ways in which it should be combated. Consider these questions:

Bullies are supposed to be cowardly, backing off if attacked themselves. Is that your experience?

Are there people who are natural victims, who seem to invite bullying? Is bullying the imposing of one personality on another? If so, is there an element of bullying in all relationships, in marriages and friendships, for instance?

Is status a cause of bullying – a foreman bullying workmen, a teacher pupils?

☐▭ ▥▷ *LANGUAGE PRACTICE*

A piece of writing to criticise

A time when I saw someone being bullied

Read this story written by a girl preparing for the GCSE examination. It appears here just as she wrote it, including her mistakes.

1 'Say thank you then,' they said to him. 'Say thank you to your kind friend, or else we're just gonna have to hurt you again, and we don't want that, do we?'

The bus rumbled on, and the journey must have seemed endless to that second-year boy. Every day it was the same; where ever James Smith sat, it
5 was always the same. One would sit next to him, two behind him, and they would remove his glasses and jab his hand with a pin and then give him a quick hard hit on his head if he did not say 'Thank you'.
They said they were teaching him manners.

Buses are ideal places for bullying, and probably one of the few places
10 where it actually does take place. There is at least a twenty-minute journy; plenty of time to reduce someone to tears, if you are a skilled bully. Your victim can-not escape and there is the added advantage of there being no adults, except the bus driver, who has seen it all before and does not care anyway.

15 On our bus many people had to stand, and it was customery for the older pupils to say 'Budge up' to younger pupils, and sit three-to-a-seat. However this did not work in reverse. James Smith made the mistake of asking two fifth years to 'budge-up' and this was just not done.
'What'd yer say? demanded one, astounded.
20 'Er, could you move up . . . please' replied James already regretting it.
'This boy needs teaching some manners,' said the other fifth year. By now the bus had become quite quiet. Every one listened. They looked out the windows or talked quietly to friends and avoided the fifth years' gaze, but they listened all the same.
25 They made him ask them the question over and over again, saying they could not hear him and he would have to speak louder, until he was shouting at them, and everyone else was laughing cruely at him.

After that the two boys and another friend who had joined them, sat behind him whenever possible. It soon became a habit to leave the two seats behind
30 James Smith empty, where ever he sat.

They started quite gentley, just kicking his chair and blowing smoke in his face until his eyes watered, or flicking ink onto his blazer, but as they realised they were having more attention from other pupils they began to enjoy themselves, enjoy the authority and power they had over the small boy. They
35 never physicly hurt him much, just the pin and the odd thump, certainly not enough to cause any long term pain. Instead they mocked, embarassed and totally demoralised him, until he spoke to no one, was frightened of everyone and did everything they commanded.

On the last day of term, the last day of school for the three fifth years, he
40 must have finally had some hope and seen an end to his misery.
    The three boys sat by him.
    'Now James, my friend, are you going to give me your glasses? We don't want them broken now, do we?' asked one of them sarcasticly.
    'No' was the reply. For the first time ever James Smith said no to them.
45 They hit him and shouted at him but he still said no.
    Finally just as we were entering the village one of them took a flask of hot tea from his bag and poured it over Jame's head as a last resort. The tea leaves caught in his fair hair, the tea trickled down his face, and his glasses steamed up.
50 The bus came to the stop and he ran off crying bitterly.
    'Maybe that'll teach you some manners' one shouted after him, just to add to his shame and distress.
    He never saw them again, as they left school. He soon began to mix with other people again.
55 Now he sits at the back of the bus smoking and kicking the first years' chairs until they thank him.

Assessment

Use this essay to practise judging your own work. Below are points examiners take into consideration. Apply them to your own work throughout the book.

Imagine you are the examiner and decide how successful this story is by answering these questions. Give reasons for your answer in each case.

Beginning

Does the writer seize your attention at the beginning of her story so that you want to read on?
Does she get straight to the point, or does she waste time at the beginning?

Setting

Does she give you a sense of the setting of the story?

Characters

Has she made her characters seem real and believable?

Structure

Is the story clearly structured, or is it muddled?
Is it easy to follow?

Ending

Is the story neatly rounded off at the end, or are you left wondering whether it
has finished?
How does she end her story?
What point is she making?

Style and expression

Is her style and expression smooth and pleasing to the ear, or is it clumsy and
awkward? Write down any clumsy or badly-expressed phrases you find.
Does she use slang or colloquialisms which are inappropriate? Write down
any that you find.

Spelling and punctuation

Is her spelling and punctuation accurate or is the story marred by many
mistakes? Write down her mistakes.

A sense of belief

Do you feel that she is writing from personal experience, or has she entirely
invented the story? How do you know?

NOTE

The essay is above average generally and would gain a high grade. Note how
the few mistakes are careless ones: always check your own writing for
accuracy.

▭ ▦▷ *EXAMINATION PRACTICE*

Read this short story and answer the questions that follow.

Gran and the Roaring Boys

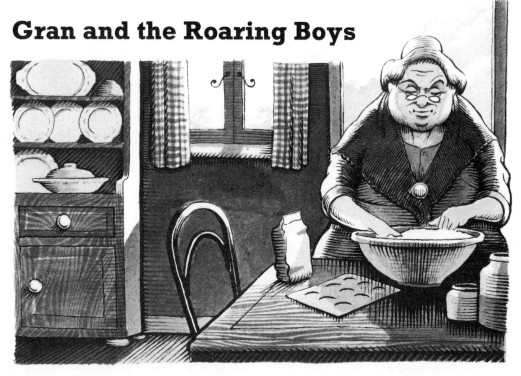

1   In some circles, it might be considered a social disadvantage to have a witch
for a grandmother. But not in Aberllyn. My Gran was nobility in Aberllyn.
Gran was an asset at any village tea-party and Gran, as often as the local GP,
was consulted in times of crisis. Mostly, of course, it was just sick cows, or
5   injured birds brought to the back doorstep, or a love potion. Very good on
warts, too, was Gran, a bit of spit, a rub with a potato cut in two, six lines of the
Old Language, and Tuesday week – no wart!

     Possibly Gran was so popular because she didn't look like a witch. The only
apparent familiars she had were Sws and me, and us part-time, being summer
10 visitors only. Gran was five feet nothing, and round as a cottage loaf above
and below the ties of her apron. Her skin was the colour of the milk left in the
churn when the butter's taken off, with a spot of colour added on each cheek
from the little pot she kept hidden down the side of her armchair. There was
nothing witchy about the house, either. Clean as a washboard, bright with
15 check curtains, wood tables scrubbed until the surface had faded to cream
and the grain rubbed soft as flannel on the palm of the hand; willow china in
quantity, and a fire glowing in the belly of the squat, blackleaded range
summer and winter. Back door never locked and flung wide all summer to the
pungent scents of the herb garden loud with bees and fluttering distracted

20   with cabbage whites and clean washing.

Not everybody, of course, believed that Gran was a witch. Good with herbs, they said, and a quaint old character, but witches, they said, don't exist. But that didn't stop Mrs Gomer Jones Very Holy sneaking into Gran's kitchen with her rheumaticky knees, nor the Chapel ladies ducking into curtsies when
25   Gran sailed into Evans Grocer.
Gran had a Reputation, and them as was wise didn't cross her. There were two that did, and they – well, better start in the morning, like Gran says, and finish at sunset.

It all happened the summer Sws turned sixteen. Nine years older than me,
30   and up until that year all scratches and slaps, except when Gran was there. 'Brothers and sisters, cats and dogs, fighters all,' our Gran used to say. 'But do it here and I will string the pair of you like runner beans.' Meant it, too, although she never actually lifted a finger to either of us. Mostly Gran was twinkles, hot scones and hugs, but cross her and it was black looks and hide if
35   you knew what was good for you!
Anyway, Sws was sixteen and me seven, and that summer we decided we liked each other. Sws was becoming very mysterious and lumpy in the front with bosoms, but for all that she would still race me up Bryn Glasllyn and duck me in the lake. But that year there was another, dark side to Sws, very quiet,
40   and thinking a lot, and looking under her lashes at the Roaring Boys. Troubled me, this side of Sws, for it shut me out; some days she wasn't interested in the lithe *sewin* barring the river inches from our fishing lines, or the frogs leaping frantic in the side pools avoiding our swarming fingers, or even the crabs scuttling sideways over our bare feet in the beach pools, Sws being too busy
45   thinking deep and chewing hair. But even thinking Sws was pretty to turn heads.
The village biddies, even, who wouldn't have had a good word for St Peter unless he turned Chapel, looked at her with softness in their button eyes when she bobbed her head and wished them *'bore da'*. Sws had a dark, intense
50   Welshness, the Celtic look of her softened by the high rose tints of my mother's Hereford English, and white teeth like the little fragments of shell we found on the beach, in a mouth that could sulk and pout, being female, but mostly smiled. But her eyes were eyes to startle, being green as Glasllyn in spring, and with Gran's way of looking into one's face as if eyes were
55   windows and the soul on show without curtains. Only no wrinkles, of course, round Sws's eyes, since Gran had plenty for both!

The Roaring Boys set eyes on Sws that year, and the village girls sulked and poked their noses in the air and bustled a lot with 'I don't cares', and made a point of ignoring the Roaring Boys, who didn't notice.
60   Twenty years each, had the Roaring Boys, being twins, and count their length in yards. Llew and Choss, fishermen's faces tanned into spider web lines round the eyes; handsome, strong, and both paid on Friday, more was the pity, since every Friday night saw them together in the Aberllyn Arms,

money that should have been in their pockets swishing in their bellies with
65 froth on top, and coming out loud in the way they bickered, and bellowed, and
shouted. A roaring, quarrelsome pair, these, and they quarrelled loudest over
Sws. Sws laughed with me and rationed them to a smile a day, although I could
tell she was a little bit pleased at all the fuss.

Gran, being Gran, missed nothing, and anyway, the Roaring Boys made no
70 secret of it, mooning under Sws's window night after night. They came to
blows under it, too, one Friday, and I scurried down to Sws's room to crouch
nosy behind the curtain and peer down on the struggling pair below. Sws
looked at me, once, and in her eyes was wonder at the madness that was in
them. Madness it seemed to me, too, since Sws was all right as sisters go, but
75 nothing, as far as I could tell, to fight over.
But suddenly Gran was out there, buckets full sloshing over the pair of them,
plaits bristling over her nightdress with indignation, chasing them into their
cottage and the bucket slung after for good measure.
Round to apologise next morning, both of them, and return the bucket,
80 puffed eyes, cut lips and all, gawking on the doorstep for a glimpse of Sws,
daft as sheep, and Gran warned them off, five foot nothing seeing to two at six
and a half, and them listening, since Grans, in our part of the world, were
people to listen to, and mine in particular for reasons already mentioned.
'You leave her, you hear?' she ordered, eyes sparkling, wagging finger
85 chopping the air. 'Sws is only sixteen, and too young for you.' Gran folded her
arms across the starched armament of her pinna and put her head back to see
up at the loft of them, squinting her eyes against the morning sun. 'You know
what people call me,' she said. 'Some laugh, but I warn you. Lay a finger on
Sws and the devil himself won't know where to hide you.'
90 The Roaring Boys shuffled their feet, scratched their heads, smirked at each
other, handed over the bucket and trooped down the path.
But Gran came very tightlipped that day, and baked two lots of scones
without slipping us even one, hot from the oven. We sat and sniffed at the
fragrant steam in anguish, since Gran with a Misery was not to be pestered
95 and them what asked didn't get.

The Roaring Boys stole Sws on Monday night. Out at seven with a jar of
embrocation for Mrs Gomer Jones Very Holy's creaky knees, delivered the
medicine and disappeared.
When our Carmarthen granfer clock chimed ten and still Sws's nose hadn't
100 come round the back door, Gran skewered her pancake hat to her bun,
wrapped her shawl round her shoulders, and went looking. Back came Gran
in half an hour, chin trembling to scare me stiff, but no Sws. She whisked me
from my nightshirt and into my trews, and tugged me flying behind down the
road for Meirion Police.
105 Policemen came very scarce around Aberllyn in those days, there being
only Meirion in a twenty mile radius, and him not averse to a sly salmon taken
from the Teifi below the Castle when the moon was ducking into cloud and the
gamekeeper firing off snores instead of two barrels.

But we found Meirion Police eventually, by a process of elimination,
110 shamefaced with his boots off in the front parlour of Mrs Waldo Rhys Atlantic
Sailor where, Gran told him sharp, he had no right to be, and better poach for
salmon than honest men's wives, especially with crime all over the place while
his back was turned.

Gran bustled Meirion Police off to look for Sws, tugged me home, fed me
115 milk and, preoccupied, sent me to bed. Twice she sent me, and three times I
crept down, peering through the banisters lonely for Sws. I sat on the knotted
rag rug at the top of the stairs and watched Gran unlock the big corner
cupboard and fetch stone pots and glass bottles; mix, burn, tie and strew, the
Old Language wafting around the rafters like steam and with a bit of special
120 Gran swearing for good measure. The flames of the fire leapt blue in the grate
with the handfuls of herbs crackling pungent on it.
   And suddenly in the firelight was Cat: erect, black and motionless to be
hardly there, wreathed in smoke like a left-over dream. Then the triangular
mask opened in a cavernous, high-barred yawn, green eyes slitting, pink
125 tongue curved and cupped delicate behind the needle teeth.

Yawns being contagious, I yawned with him, blinked once, and Cat was
gone.
   Deeply regretful I felt for the Roaring Boys.
   Meirion Police brought back our Sws at four in the morning. Gran said
130 *'diolch'*, shut the door in his curious face, and bustled us to bed. I crept in with
Sws for comfort and company, and we lay spooned together for what
remained of the night.

Nobody ever saw the Roaring Boys again, although Meirion Police sleuthed all over Aberllyn, very serious, with licked pencil and a new notebook.

135 I never saw Cat again, either, but he came back just once after the house slept, because Tuesday morning there were two dead rats on Gran's Blaenau slate back doorstep, big black ones, side by side, all nice and tidy, with inches of scaly tails and long yellow teeth poking from half-open mouths. I wanted to keep them, being partial to a bit of nature study on a dull morning, but Gran

140 clipped my ear, said *'Ach-y-fi'* and buried them under the blackcurrant bush by the tybach.

Jenny Sullivan

NOTE

sewin are salmon trout
bore da means good morning
diolch means thank you
Ach-y-fi is an expression of disgust

Understanding and directed writing

1 Say how far you agree or disagree with each of these statements about the story. Give evidence from the story to support your answers.

a) There was 'nothing witchy' about Gran. (lines 8–20)
b) Sws 'shut out' her younger brother from her life. (lines 29–46)
c) Sws was probably willing to be 'stolen' by the Roaring Boys.

2 Write one sentence about each of these short extracts from the passage explaining the writer's full meaning. Consider, in each case, whether the writer means to imply more than she actually says.

a) 'The village biddies, even, who wouldn't have had a good word for St Peter unless he turned Chapel...' (lines 47–48)
b) 'the village girls sulked... and made a point of ignoring the Roaring Boys, who didn't notice.' (lines 57–59)
c) 'the gamekeeper firing off snores instead of two barrels' (line 108)

3 Re-read lines 114–141 and decide

a) what evidence you would offer against Gran if you were prosecuting her for practising witchcraft.
b) what defence you would offer against the charges. (Consider why most of the boys' evidence might be suspect.)

Write about 80 words for the prosecution and about 60 words in Gran's defence.

4 Perhaps the only really mysterious aspect of the story is the disappearance of the Roaring Boys. Write half a page giving a logical explanation for their disappearance.

2 The language of selling

This section studies the methods, language and style of the business world of buying and selling.

You are asked to

→ Re-organise and interpret information from a character sketch

→ Discuss and analyse the appropriateness of vocabulary and style

→ Examine the work of an advertising agency

→ Write advertisements in language appropriate for selling a particular product

→ Study closely the language of a number of advertisements

→ Take the roles of salesperson and customer

Examination practice – fill in a form and write a formal letter

SOCK IT TO 'EM IN 1930

The Grapes of Wrath

'The Grapes of Wrath' by John Steinbeck tells of the plight of the people of Oklahoma, driven from their farms by large landowners to look for work in California. They needed cars to reach California and so used car lots sprang up all over Oklahoma.

Read this description of a typical used car lot, seen mainly through the eyes of the owner.

1   Those sons-of-bitches over there ain't buying. Every yard gets 'em. They're lookers. Spend all their time looking. Don't want to buy no cars; take up your time. Don't give a damn for your time. Over there, them two people – no, with the kids. Get 'em in a car. Start 'em at two hundred and work down. They look
5   good for one and a quarter. Get 'em rolling. Get 'em out in a jalopy. Sock it to 'em! They took our time.
　　Owners with rolled-up sleeves. Salesmen, neat, deadly, small intent eyes watching for weaknesses.
　　Watch the woman's face. If the woman likes it we can screw the old man.
10   Start 'em on that Cad'. Then you can work 'em down to that '26 Buick. 'F you start on the Buick, they'll go for a Ford. Roll up your sleeves an' get to work. This ain't gonna last forever. Show 'em that Nash while I get the slow leak pumped up on that '25 Dodge.

　　What you want is transportation, ain't it? No baloney for you. Sure the
15   upholstery is shot. Seat cushions ain't turning no wheels over.

　　Cars lined up, noses forward, rusty noses, flat tyres. Parked close together.

　　Like to get in to see that one? Sure, no trouble. I'll pull her out of the line.

　　Get 'em under obligation. Make 'em take up your time. Don't let 'em forget they're takin' your time. People are nice, mostly. They hate to put you out.
20   Make 'em put you out, an' then sock it to 'em.
　　Flags, red and white, white and blue – all along the kerb. Used Cars. Good Used Cars.
　　To-day's bargain – up on the platform. Never sell it. Makes folks come in, though. If we sold that bargain at that price we'd hardly make a dime. Tell 'em
25   it's jus' sold. Take out that yard battery before you make delivery. Put in that dumb cell. Christ, what they want for six bits? Roll up your sleeves – pitch in. This ain't gonna last. If I had enough jalopies I'd retire in six months.

　　Listen, Jim, I heard that Chevvy's rear end. Sounds like bustin' bottles. Squirt in a couple quarts of sawdust. Put some in the gears too. We got to
30   move that lemon for thirty-five dollars. Bastard cheated me on that one. I offer ten an' he jerks me to fifteen, an' then the son-of-a-bitch took the tools out. God

Almighty! I wisht I had five hundred jalopies. This ain't gonna last. He don't like the tyres? Tell 'im they got ten thousand in 'em, knock off a buck an' a half.
See if you can't find a spark plug that ain't cracked. Christ, if I had fifty
35 trailers at under a hundred I'd clean up. What the hell is he kickin' about? We sell 'em, but we don't push 'em home for him. That's good! Don't push 'em home. Get that one in the Monthly, I bet. You don't think he's a prospect? Well, kick 'im out. We got too much to do to bother with a guy that can't make up his mind. Take the right front tyre off the Graham. Turn that mended side down.
40 The rest looks swell. Got tread an' everything.

Hot sun on rusted metal. Oil on the ground. People are wandering in, bewildered, needing a car.

Wipe your feet. Don't lean on that car, it's dirty. How do you buy a car? What does it cost? Watch the children now. I wonder how much for this one?
45 We'll ask. It don't cost money to ask. We can ask, can't we? Can't pay a nickel over seventy-five, or there won't be enough to get to California.

God, if I could only get a hundred jalopies. I don't care if they run or not.
All right, Joe. You soften 'em up and shoot 'em in here. I'll close 'em, I'll deal 'em or I'll kill 'em. Don't send in no bums. I want deals.

50   Yes, sir, step in. You got a buy there. Yes, sir! At eighty bucks you got a buy.

I can't go no higher than fifty. The fella outside says fifty.

Fifty. Fifty? He's nuts. Paid seventy-eight fifty for that little number. Joe, you crazy fool, you tryin' to bust us? Have to can that guy. I might take sixty. Now
55 look here, mister, I ain't got all day. I'm a business man but I ain't out to stick nobody. Got anything to trade?

Got a pair of mules I'll trade.

Mules! Hey, Joe, hear this? This guy wants to trade mules. Didn't nobody tell you this is the machine age? They don't use mules for nothing but glue no
60 more.

Fine big mules – five and seven years old. Maybe we better look around.

Look around! You come in when we're busy, an' take up our time an' then walk out! Joe, did you know you was talkin' to pikers?

I ain't a piker. I got to get a car. We're goin' to California. I got to get a car.
65 Well, I'm a sucker. Joe says I'm a sucker. Says if I don't quit givin' my shirt away I'll starve to death. Tell you what I'll do – I can get five bucks apiece for them mules for dog feed.

I wouldn't want them to go for dog feed.

Well, maybe I can get ten or seven maybe. Tell you what we'll do. We'll
70 take your mules for twenty. Wagon goes with 'em, don't it? An' you put up fifty, an' you can sign a contract to send the rest at ten dollars a month.

But you said eighty.

Didn't you never hear about carrying charges and insurance? That just boosts her a little. You'll get her all paid up in four-five months. Sign your
75 name right here. We'll take care of ever'thing.

Well, I don't know –

Now, look here. I'm givin' you my shirt, an' you took all this time. I might a made three sales while I been talkin' to you. I'm disgusted. Yeah, sign right there. All right, sir. Joe, fill up the tank for this gentleman. We'll give him
80 petrol.

Jesus, Joe, that was a hot one! What'd we give for that jalopy? Thirty bucks – thirty-five wasn't it? I got that team, an' if I can't get seventy-five for that team, I ain't a business man. An' I got fifty cash an' a contract for forty more. Oh, I know they're not all honest, but it'll surprise you how many kick through with
85 the rest. One guy come through with a hundred two years after I wrote him off. I bet you this guy sends the money. Christ, if I could only get five hundred jalopies! Roll up your sleeves, Joe. Go out an' soften 'em, an' send 'em in to me. You get twenty on that last deal. You ain't doing bad.

Limp flags in the afternoon sun. To-day's Bargain. '29 Ford pickup, runs
90 good.

What do you want for fifty bucks – a Zephyr?

Horsehair curling out of seat cushions, fenders battered and hammered back. Bumpers torn loose and hanging. Fancy Ford roadster with little coloured lights at fender guide, at radiator cap, and three behind. Mud
95 aprons, and a big die on the gear-shift lever. Pretty girl on tyre cover, painted in colour and named Cora. Afternoon sun on the dusty windshields.

Christ, I ain't had time to go out an' eat! Joe, send a kid for a hamburger.

Spattering roar of ancient engines.

100 There's a dumb bunny lookin' at that Chrysler. Find out if he got any jack in his jeans. Some a these farm boys is sneaky. Soften 'em up an' roll 'em in to me, Joe. You're doin' good.

Sure, we sold it. Guarantee? We guaranteed it to be an automobile. We didn't guarantee to wet-nurse it. Now listen here, you – you bought a car, an'
105 now you're squawkin'. I don't give a damn if you don't make payments. We ain't got your paper. We turn that over to the finance company. They'll get after you, not us. We don't hold no paper. Yeah? Well you jus' get tough an' I'll call a cop. No, we did not switch the tyres. Run 'im outa here, Joe. He bought a car, an' now he ain't satisfied. How'd you think if I bought a steak an' et half an' try to bring it back? We're runnin' a business, not a charity ward. Can ya
110 imagine that?

John Steinbeck

Understanding the passage

NOTE

Three of the questions below ask you to extract, organise and interpret information from the passage. You might find it useful to make numbered notes of the information you wish to use before making your summary.

lines 1–20

1 In about 50 words explain how the salesman's method is based on his judgment of people's characters.
2 Explain the irony in
a) Sure, no trouble. (line 17)
b) People are nice, mostly. (line 19)

lines 21–47

1 In about 50 words explain the various methods of cheating used by the salesman.
2 What repeatedly expressed regret does the salesman have?
3 What do you think the *Monthly* is? (line 37)
What does the salesman want to put in the *Monthly*?
What does this show about his attitude to the customers?
4 What does the writer show about the customers in lines 43–46?

The language of selling

lines 48–88

1 'You soften 'em up an' shoot 'em in here. I'll close 'em, I'll deal 'em or I'll kill
'em.'
Explain how the writer shows this process in his description of what happens
to the man with the mules. Use 80–100 words.

lines 102–110

1 The impression of the used car lot has been given almost entirely through the
salesman's words. In this section he is answering a customer's complaints.
Interpret from the salesman's words the complaints and threats the customer is
making.

Discussion

The Grapes of Wrath was written in 1939.
   Compare the type of selling shown in the extract with selling today. Begin
with anecdotes from several people about their own or their families'
experiences and then consider:
What differences and similarities are there?
Have salespersons changed?
Have new laws helped to protect customers?
Are the customers different from those described in the passage?
Are there other laws that you would introduce to protect customers?
Do salespersons need some protection nowadays from the false claims of
customers? Consider, for instance, how many people have returned clothes to
shops having already worn them.

Vocabulary and style

Compare lines 1–3 with this version.

   'Every yard has people such as those over there who spend all their time
   looking and never buy, people who waste your time and who never intend
   to buy your cars.'

What is the difference in sentence structure and vocabulary?

Why are the short sentences and colloquial expressions in the original version
suitable for the salesman's character?

Re-write lines 9–13 in only three sentences and without the colloquial
expressions. What has been lost from the original version?

Character

The style of the passage suits the character of the salesman – fast-talking, confident, pleased with his cleverness.

In a passage of about 100 words try the same method to give the impression of *either* a market trader *or* a guide showing people round a tourist sight.

Include comments that make the audience's response clear. For example, 'I'd be grateful if your son would keep his hands off ornaments, madam.'

You may if you wish include asides by the speaker such as, 'Antique writing desks are definitely the best line, Jim.' 'I can sell 'em much faster than you can make them.'

SOCK IT TO 'EM IN 1986
SHELL GOLD CARD

Modern selling is often done through advertising agencies. This is one agency's suggested method of selling.

The product the advertising agency has been asked to sell is the *Shell Gold Card.*

The card is used by drivers of company cars. The drivers buy petrol, and have their cars serviced and repaired with the Shell Gold Card. They sign sales vouchers which are then sent to Shell.

Membership of the AA is included.

The benefits of the Gold Card are:

1 The customer avoids having many invoices from different garages. One invoice for all the company's cars arrives each month.
2 Each driver's bill is shown separately and the mileage is recorded by the garage. The company can check the performance of each car and each driver.

The agency decided to advertise on radio.

They prepared the three 40-second advertisements on pages 42 and 43.

Three radio advertisements

NOTE

MV means male voice.
FX means sound effects.

Donkeywork

MV: Company car fleets create an awful lot of donkeywork.

(*FX: Hee-haw of donkey*)

Thousands of petrol receipts, expenses claims and garage accounts.

(*FX: Hee-haw*)

Endless cheque-writing and VAT calculating.

(*FX: Hee-haw*)

But Shell Gold Card gets rid of all this costly administration.

Shell Gold Card is the complete car fleet management system.

Your drivers can refuel without cash throughout the UK and you receive just one monthly invoice.

VAT is shown separately.

Servicing and repairs can be included too.

And the monthly Shell Gold Card cost analysis shows which cars are running well,

and which ones . . .

(*FX: Hee-haw*)

. . . are the donkeys.

The Shell Gold Card system.

Ask at any Shell station.

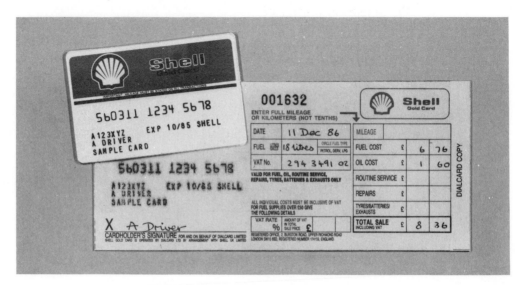

Clanger

MV: With a company car fleet, it's so easy to drop a clanger.
Was it a mistake to buy foreign cars?
(*FX: Boing!!!*)
Are your Cavaliers more economical than your Sierras?
(*FX: Boing!!!*)
Do automatics cost less in the long run?
(*FX: Boing!!!*)
Shell Gold Card gives you the information you need.
Because Shell Gold Card is the complete fleet management system.
There's a detailed monthly analysis, monitoring every car's movements and costs.
Plus nationwide fuel purchase without cash, covered by a single monthly invoice.
Shell Gold Card saves fleet management time, cuts operating costs . . .
(*FX: Boing!!!*)
. . . and helps avoid expensive clangers.
The Shell Gold Card system.
Ask at any Shell station.

Mr Heavyfoot

MV: Every company car fleet has a Mr Heavyfoot.
(*FX: Engine revving*)
Put him in a company car, and his right foot becomes *very* heavy.
(*FX: Fast acceleration*)
So he uses more petrol.
Wears out tyres and brake linings.
(*FX: Heavy braking*)
And costs you more money.
Now, who's the Mr Heavyfoot in *your* fleet?
A Shell Gold Card monthly analysis would tell you at a glance.
Shell Gold Card is the complete car fleet management system.
Your drivers can refuel without cash throughout the UK and you receive just one monthly invoice.
Servicing and repairs can be included too.
And the Shell Gold Card analysis sorts out the wrong cars from the right . . .
(*FX: Engine revving*)
. . . and the heavy feet from the light!
The Shell Gold Card system.
Ask at any Shell station.

Analysing the advertisements

In a paragraph of 60–80 words explain the different aims of the advertisements. Which advantage of the Gold Card is each stressing? How do they make different uses of sound effects?

Writing 1

Write a script for a Shell Gold Card TV advertisement, using one of the three ideas from the radio script or making up one of your own.

TV scripts have to be strikingly visual. Below is an example from an advertisement for a camera, the Samson. The advertisers have decided to use a gymnast and to show off the different programmes of the camera by taking action shots.

The visual part of the advertisement is on the left and the accompanying commentary is on the right. Of course the two have to match – the opening shot is of the camera's trade name with no sound.

Vision	Sound
Open with shot of Samson logo	1½ seconds silence
	MVO The Samson 2000
Cut to film loading in the camera	A built-in motor loads automatically
Cut to gymnast warming up	Three programmes are available for the camera
The gymnast tenses	Standard
Screen switches wide	Wide
Cut to gymnast leaping horse	and Tele

NOTE

MVO means Male Voice Over.
A *logo* is the design or emblem used to represent a company.
Cut means switch the camera to another shot.

Writing 2

Now write the script for either a radio or TV advertisement for one of these products.

1 A tennis racket with unbreakable strings. It is 20 per cent more expensive than most rackets of the same quality. Invent a suitable name. How will you mention the extra cost?
2 A new chocolate bar with dark chocolate one end and milk chocolate the other. Invent a suitable name.

Vocabulary

An advertisement for lager shows a man in old-fashioned dress sitting in beautiful countryside trying to write a poem. His first line is

'I walked about a bit on my own'

He sighs and tries again.

'I went around without anybody else'

He says *Oh, no!* and sits and drinks the lager.

Now he writes

'I wandered lonely as a cloud
That floats on high o'er vales and hills'

Who is the man? What is the poem?

Write a failed version

Write a 'failed' version for each of these famous lines.

> 'If music be the food of love, play on'

> 'Oh, to be in England
> Now that April's here'

> 'Ah, what can ail thee, Knight at arms
> Alone and palely loitering'

> 'Friends, Romans, Countrymen, lend me your ears'

Compare your efforts. Why do most versions sound comical?

▭▦▷ *LANGUAGE PRACTICE*

The language of advertising

The words used in an advertisement are called *copy*. A copywriter must maintain a balance between:

a) making the product seem as appealing and attractive as possible, and
b) making claims for the product which cannot be proved to be false.

Questions on four advertisements

Study the copy of the advertisements on pages 47, 48 and 49 and answer the following questions:

1 List the words and phrases which are chosen to make the products sound attractive.
2 How do the sherry and Bang and Olufsen advertisements make you feel that you are being given the facts and taken into the advertisers' confidence?
3 Collect examples of the use of questions. What effect are they intended to have?
4 What words do the advertisers of Bang and Olufsen and Venice Simplon Orient-Express use to protect themselves from misleading the consumer about their prices?
5 The sherry and Philishave advertisements use very short sentences, whereas the Bang and Olufsen advertisement uses very long ones. What is the effect in each case?

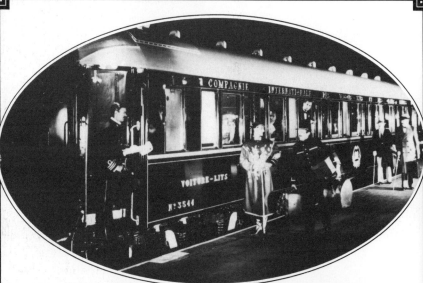

Everything you dreamed TV could be.

No doubt you have already designed your ideal video system. The perfect combination of TV and video recorder that has everything, does everything, is easy to use, highly reliable, looks and sounds marvellous, and won't become obsolete the minute you buy it.

Did you include multiple connection possibilities for your home computer, video disc player, video games console, sound recorder, headphones, hi-fi system and extension speaker to save all that plugging and unplugging?

What about the control system? Is your VCR operated by the same infra-red remote control keypad as the TV? Does it use the popular VHS format and include a 14-day, 5-programme timer? Can it record and play back in stereo? Has it got tape-scan and freeze-frame?

And your TV – is the picture perfect, the colour clear and natural? Is the sound true high-fidelity, with bass and treble controls and stereo capability?

Does your blue-print include a computerised search-and-store tuning system that covers the entire UHF band and has memory capacity for over 30 channels? Did you choose the advanced 30AX in-line High Bright tube?

Snap! This proves that great minds really do think alike. Because your idea of the perfect video system is exactly the same as ours.

The only difference is that yours is still just a dream while ours is already a fact. And ours includes some options, like Teletext, a choice of mono or stereo-capable TV's, 20", 22" or 26" screens, rich teak or rosewood finish or a modern, hard-wearing matt grey. There's a choice of price too, with TV's starting from about £400 and videos from about £600.

Go and see your dream in action at your nearest Bang & Olufsen dealer. Or fill in its finer details by contacting us, Bang & Olufsen UK Limited, Dept. P 2, Eastbrook Road, Gloucester GL4 7DE. Telephone (0452) 21591.

Bang & Olufsen

Role-play

The extracts in this chapter have shown that modern selling is more subtle than fifty years ago. Few people nowadays, for instance, would be bullied into buying by accusations of wasting the salesperson's time.

In pairs, take turns at being a door-to-door salesperson and a customer. Try two different products and two different approaches each. Prepare your sales approach beforehand, but do not let your partner know your product or your method until he or she 'answers the door'.

Remember it is not a competition. You are acting parts, so you have not been defeated if you buy the product.

Discussion

Discuss what you discovered about the best salesperson approaches and customer responses. Some pairs could demonstrate their encounters to the rest of the class.

Writing

Write an essay in which you present the arguments for and against the present level of advertising in our society.

▷ *EXAMINATION PRACTICE*

Directed writing

You have decided to join a tennis, squash or badminton club after school. Your parents approve and buy you a racket. Write, in about 25 lines, the conversation in which you try to persuade them that you need a new sweat-shirt or T-shirt, a pair of gym or tennis shoes and probably a tracksuit.

Filling in an order form

Imagine you have persuaded your parents that you need at least two of the items. Using the section of the brochure opposite, copy out and complete the order form for the articles.

Track Suits

Minimum order three per size, same colour.

P4 Polyester Top Red, royal, black or navy with 2 white stripes down sleeves. Trousers — tapered leg with stirrup and 2 white stripes down legs.
26"/28" *TUF 128* £10.73, 30"/32" *TUF 132* £11.30
34" *TUF 134* £12.78, 36" *TUF 136* £14.53
38" *TUF 138* £15.11, 40" *TUF 140* £15.11
42" *TUF 142* £15.11

P5 Polyester Top With black/red, navy/green or navy/saxe panel. Trousers — plain with straight legs.
26"/28" *TUF 228* £10.87, 30"/32" *TUF 232* £10.87
34" *TUF 234* £12.63, 36" *TUF 236* £14.52
38" *TUF 238* £15.11, 40" *TUF 240* £15.11
42" *TUF 242* £15.11

Track Trousers

Polyester with plain leg, elasticated waist.
Colours: black or navy.
Extra Small *FRF 001T* £4.97, **Small** *FRF 002T* £6.06
Medium *FRF 003T* £6.80, **Large** *FRF 004T* £7.16

Sweat Shirts

Cotton Fleece Backed
Plain colours: red, sky, navy, royal, black, gold, white.
30" *TUF 530* £4.52, 32" *TUF 532* £4.52
34" *TUF 534* £4.52, 36" *TUF 536* £4.52
38" *TUF 538* £4.52, 40" *TUF 540* £4.52

Sweat Shirts — Printed

Price per garment with print. Minimum quantity 10.
30" *TUF 730* £4.85, 32" *TUF 732* £4.85
34" *TUF 734* £4.85, 36" *TUF 736* £4.85
38" *TUF 738* £4.85, 40" *TUF 740* £4.85

Screen printing charge (any quantity, screen can be re-used on subsequent orders)   **£25.00**

T-Shirts — Printed

Price per garment with print.
Minimum quantity 12.

XS	*TUF 330* **£2.45**		S	*TUF 334* **£2.45**
M	*TUF 338* **£2.45**		L	*TUF 340* **£2.45**
XL	*TUF 342* **£2.45**			

Screen printing charge (screen can be re-used on subsequent orders)   **£25.00**

Footwear Price per pair

Tennis Shoes

Burton Green Zap
Canvas upper, "Herring Bone" moulded rubber sole
Small Sizes 3 - 5   *FTF 561* **£7.45**
Large Sizes 6 - 11   *FTF 562* **£7.45**

Gym Shoes

Supersport Gym slippers with suede sole
Sizes 11 - 2   *FTG 112* **£2.17**
Sizes 3 - 5   *FTG 350* **£2.40**
Sizes 6 - 11   *FTG 611* **£2.40**

Order Form
M.T. Evans & Son (The Sports People) Ltd.

Churchfields Industrial Estate
Hadham HL1 3PQ, England   Telephone (0701) 629931

Quantity	Code	Description	Price
		Total	

From

Name	Signed
Address	
	Date
Telephone No.	

PLEASE REMEMBER TO FILL IN YOUR NAME AND ADDRESS PREFERABLY IN BLOCK LETTERS. It will help us to avoid mistakes if you use the ARTICLE CODE.

Writing a letter of complaint

After two games, you find your gym/tennis shoes are defective. Write a letter of complaint, giving all the relevant details, and asking for the shoes to be replaced or your money refunded.

3   Build up a report

Schools ancient and modern

This section shows a method of building a longer piece of work by examining evidence of conditions and methods in schools a hundred years ago and contrasting them with schools of today.

You are asked to

————————→ **Draw conclusions about students, teaching methods and discipline in schools a hundred years ago**

————————→ **Contrast them with schools of today**

————————→ **Make a record of your impressions of your own schooldays**

————————→ **Explore through role-play the contrasts between Victorian and present-day schools**

————————→ **Study and practise the use of the comma**

Examination practice – answer questions on a poem

SCHOOLS A HUNDRED YEARS AGO

Examining evidence

What were schools like a hundred years ago? Use these extracts from:

a) school books of the time
b) diaries or records of people's experiences
c) students' recollections
d) novels

as the basis for topic or course work.

Making notes

As you read each piece you will need to make notes to prepare for your writing tasks at the end. Set out your page under the three headings shown below. The first notes under each heading have been done for you.

Schools a hundred years ago

Conditions of schools and pupils	*Methods of teaching*	*Discipline*
Charles Booth – only one washed pupil in the school he visited 'stunted growth' 'old faces' Missiles thrown at teachers by parents – children needed to work at home.	Question and answer lessons on objects e.g. glass, finding its qualities. Children's responses written into lesson plan. Sound like parrots e.g. 'What can you see out of the window?' – 'We see the garden.'	Generally noisy atmosphere – children chanting, teachers shouting. Kept in for not following reading. Jane Walsh – strapped in school for missing Mass on Sunday – kept in by mother because only clothes were being washed. Double strapping for arguing.

Lesson 1 – Glass

(This extract is from a book of instructions for teachers.)

A piece of glass should be passed round the children.

Teacher What is this which I hold in my hand?

Children A piece of glass.

Teacher Can you spell the word *glass*?
(The teacher then writes the word *glass* upon the slate and shows it to the class.)
You have all examined this glass; what do you observe? What can you say that it is?

Children It is bright.
(The teacher having written the word *qualities*, writes under it – *It is bright*.)

Teacher Take it in your hand and *feel* it.

Children It is cold.
(Written on the board under the former quality.)

Teacher Feel it again and compare it with the piece of sponge that is tied to your slate, and then tell me what you perceive in the glass.

Children It is smooth – it is hard.

Teacher What other glass is there in the room?

Children The windows.

Teacher Look out at the window and tell me what you see.

Children We see the garden.

Teacher (Closes the shutters)
Look out again, and tell what you observe.

Children We cannot see anything.

Teacher Why cannot you see anything?

Children We cannot see through the shutters.

Teacher What difference do you observe between the shutters and the glass?

Children We cannot see through the shutters, but we can through the glass.

Teacher Can you tell me any word that will express this quality which you observe in the glass?

Children No.

Teacher I will tell you, then; pay attention, that you may recollect it. It is *transparent*.

Discussion

This is a typical 'object lesson' – learning the qualities of objects. What would a modern teacher think of having lessons set out for him or her like this? What might go wrong in this lesson? Is learning the qualities of objects important?

A classroom today

An elementary school in the 1880s where all activities were carried out in the same hall. Children took it in turns to do physical exercises to keep warm.

The next two lessons are set out with the teacher's question followed by the students' reply, chanted as a whole class.

Lesson 2 – History

Who was Henry VIII?
Son of Henry VII.

What was his character?
As a young man he was bluff, generous, right royal and very handsome.

How was he when he grew older?
He was bloated, vain, cruel and selfish.

How many wives did Henry VIII marry?
Six.

What became of them?
Two he put away, two he beheaded, one died and one outlived him.

Discussion

How is fact and opinion mixed here?

Lesson 3 – Geography

The counties of England

How are Great Britain and Ireland divided?
Into counties.

How many counties are there in each?
Fifty-two in England and Wales, thirty-three in Scotland and thirty-two in Ireland.

How may the number of counties in England and Wales be remembered?
It is the same as the number of weeks in a year.

Who divided England into counties?
Alfred the Great.

For what purposes?
That persons might more easily refer to places, and that order might be more easily preserved.

Build up a report. Schools ancient and modern

How may the counties of England be grouped?
Into northern, southern, and midland.

How many are grouped in the north?
Six.

Name the three to the east or right-hand.
North-umber-land, Durham, and York.

Name the three to the west or left-hand.
Cumberland, Westmore-land, and Lancashire.

Discussion

What facts have you learnt from this lesson? How important are they? Are there other ways of learning facts?

Four comments from the time

One or two are tidy-looking boys; one has a clean washed face and a white collar on. The rest are ragged, ill-kempt, and squalid in appearance. Some are filthy dirty, others sickly looking with sore eyes and unwholesome aspect. One or two seem hopelessly dull, almost vacant. In the girls' department it is the same. Everywhere we are met by tokens of penury (poverty) and bad conditions at home. Children are pointed to us stunted in growth, with faces old beyond their years.

Life and Labour of the London Poor, Charles Booth, 1902

I well remember how, in my early career as a teacher, I had to evade sundry missiles thrown at me by irate parents who would rather have had their children running errands and washing up things in the home than wasting their time in school on such a thing as learning. Suppose the Education Act of 1870 had been decided by popular opinion, we should still be waiting for our schools to be built.

The Referendum, Women Teachers' Franchise Union Pamphlet

Tens of thousands of children in our schools are, I regret to say, grossly ignorant and utterly uninstructed, and the only thing we can do is to look to their cleanliness and give them habits of order, and promote their regular attendance, and then leave the question of results.

Chairman of the London School Board, 1870

Seventy or eighty pupils in a class are common. Sometimes there is more than one class in a room . . . many of the schools are in noisy thoroughfares . . . the teachers soon acquire the habit of shouting or, as is frequently admitted, of screaming at their pupils.

London School Board Report, 1889

Draw conclusions from these four extracts about the students' conditions, the attitude to school and the limited aims of the school authorities.

Students' recollections

The chief business of the infants was to learn to chant the alphabet and the numbers to one hundred. In the next class they chanted tables and recited the even numbers and the odd. When the children were unbearably fidgety ('fidget' was the word spoken most often by the teachers), Charlie would tell them to sit up straight; when he could hear a pin drop they should say their rhyme again. He would drop a pin and pretend he heard, through the hubbub of six classes, and then the children would chant all together Charlie's own poem, waving their hands to mark the rhythm,

Infants never must be lazy
On to work and up-si-daisy.

Right up the school, through all the six standards (there was a special class of a few boys and one or two girls above this) you did almost nothing except reading, writing and arithmetic. What a noise there used to be! Several children would be reading aloud, teachers scolding, infants reciting, all waxing louder and louder until the master rang the bell on his desk and the noise slid down to a lower note and less volume.

Reading was worst; sums you did at least write on your slate, whereas you might wait the whole half-hour of a reading lesson while boys and girls who could not read stuck at every word. If you took your finger from the word that was being read you were punished by staying in when the others went home.

Enough about the school! One was always glad to get out of it, my father said. But that was a complex, vexing business, getting out. All the children in a class came out together – or rather in order – to a series of commands. One! and you stood in your desk. Two! and you put your left leg over the seat. Three! and the right joined it. Four! you faced the land between the classes. Five! you marched on the spot. Six! You stepped forward and the pupil-teacher chanted, 'left, right, left, right, left, right.'

Mabel Ashby

NOTE

Charlie would be an older pupil – a pupil-teacher – sent by the master to teach the infants.

Every morning the priest came to each class, and asked us who had missed Mass the day before. I, and a few like me, always had to miss because Sunday was washing day, and we only had one lot of clothes.

So week by week we admitted our absence, and were given the strap for it. We should have been able to explain, but we just couldn't bother to make the effort, and we were ashamed to give the real reason. It was easier to come forward and get strapped on the hand instead.

Once – just once – I answered back.

'Don't you know,' asked the priest, 'that God loves you, and wants to see you in His house on Sundays?'

'But if He loves us, why does He want us to get the strap on Mondays if we can't go?' I asked.

I don't remember what the priest said, but I do know I got a double lot of straps when he'd gone.

Jane Walsh

It was so easy to get a beating for one thing. Some boys couldn't get through a day without 'holding out their hands', or a week without a real thrashing . . . While a thrashing proceeded, the school simmered. Would a boy cry? Was the master hitting harder than usual? It might be oneself soon. The master never caned a girl, no matter how maddening she might be.

Mabel Ashby

My word, if the teacher caught any of us doing this, the punishment was to kneel on the hard, rough floorboards, with your back upright and your hands placed on the back of your neck, for a long period of about 20 minutes. Should you lop over, aching all over, the teacher would slap you across the head with his hand and shout sternly, 'Get upright, will you?'

Albert Paul

I was kept waiting at the firm with the result that I was late. The only boy in the school to be late. I was humiliated in front of 300 boys by the Head and afterwards got six mighty slashes on the fingers with a thin cane. My God, it hurt, believe me. And something else which hurt even more. My name was inserted in the disgrace and punishment book and put on record for future reference.

Arthur Newton

Draw conclusions about the children's feelings towards school and the attitudes of the teachers to the children.

TWO NOVELISTS' VIEWS

Hard Times

1 Thomas Gradgrind, sir. A man of fact and calculations. A man who proceeds
upon the principle that two and two are four, and nothing over, and who is not
to be talked into allowing for anything over. Thomas Gradgrind, sir, with a
rule and a pair of scales, and the multiplication table always in his pocket, sir,
5 ready to weigh and measure any parcel of human nature, and tell you exactly
what it comes to. It is a mere question of figures, a case of simple arithmetic.

In such terms Mr Gradgrind always mentally introduced himself to the little
pitchers before him, who were to be filled so full of facts.

'Girl number twenty,' said Mr Gradgrind, squarely pointing with his square
10 forefinger. 'Give me your definition of a horse.'
Sissy Jupe thrown into the greatest alarm by this demand.

'Girl number twenty unable to define a horse!' said Mr Gradgrind, for the
general behoof of all the little pitchers. 'Girl number twenty possessed of no
facts, in reference to one of the commonest of animals! Some boy's definition of
15 a horse. Bitzer, yours.'

'Quadruped. Graminivorous. Forty teeth, namely twenty-four grinders, four
eye-teeth, and twelve incisors. Sheds coat in the spring; in marshy countries,
sheds hoofs too. Hoofs hard, but requiring to be shod with iron. Age known by
marks in mouth.'
20 Thus (and much more) Bitzer.

'Now girl number twenty,' said Mr Gradgrind. 'You know what a horse is.'

Charles Dickens

NOTE

Sissy Jupe's father works in a horse-riding stables.
She has lived and worked with horses all her life.

Understanding the passage

What feelings has Dickens about Thomas Gradgrind?
What types of lessons are being mocked?
What is not being taken account of in the lesson?
Comment on the title, the name of the teacher,
the use of such phrases as *Girl number twenty*,
little pitchers and Bitzer's definition of a horse.

The History of Mr Polly

1   He went first to a National School, which was run on severely economical lines
to keep down the rates, by a largely untrained staff; he was set sums to do that
he did not understand, and that no one made him understand; he was made to
read the Catechism and Bible with the utmost industry and an entire disregard
5   of punctuation or significance; caused to imitate writing copies and drawing
copies; given object-lessons upon sealing-wax and silk-worms and potato
bugs and ginger and iron and such-like things; taught various other subjects
his mind refused to entertain; and afterwards, when he was about twelve, he
was jerked by his parents to 'finish off' in a private school of dingy aspect and
10   still dingier pretensions, where there were no object lessons, and the studies
of book-keeping and French were pursued (but never effectually undertaken)
under the guidance of an elderly gentleman, who wore a nondescript gown,
and took snuff, wrote copperplate, explained nothing, and used a cane with
remarkable dexterity and gusto.

15   Mr Polly went into the National School at six, and he left the private school at
fourteen, and by that time his mind was in much the same state that you would
be in, dear reader, if you were operated upon for appendicitis by a well-
meaning, boldly enterprising but rather overworked and underpaid butcher
boy, who was superseded towards the climax of the operation by a left-
20   handed clerk of high principles but intemperate habits – that is to say, it was in
a thorough mess. The nice little curiosities and willingness of a child were in a
jumbled and thwarted condition, hacked and cut about – the operators had
left, so to speak, all their sponges and ligatures in the mangled confusion – and
Mr Polly had lost much of his natural confidence, so far as figures and sciences
25   and languages and the possibilities of learning things were concerned. He
thought of the present world no longer as a wonderland of experiences, but as
geography and history, as the repeating of names that were hard to
pronounce, and lists of products and populations and heights and lengths, and
as lists and dates – oh! and Boredom indescribable.

H G Wells

Understanding the passage

How does H G Wells suggest that Mr Polly's schooling has damaged him for
life?
What types of lessons and teachers are being attacked?
How helpful is the metaphor about the operation for making Wells' point?

Writing

These extracts can be the basis of pieces of writing of different types, suitable for collecting together as a project or coursework.

A report

Prepare a report about 400 words long on one or more of the following topics about schools a hundred years ago. Imagine that you are writing for someone who has not seen the material you have read.

    The types of lessons
    The condition and attitude of students
    The teachers
    The discipline

Refer to, or quote, pieces from the passages.

An object lesson

Write an object lesson similar to *Glass* on page 55. You might try an animal because object lessons on animals were popular, as shown in Dickens' extract.

A comic object lesson

This could be of several types. For instance, what if the children did not answer their cues?

FOR EXAMPLE:
    What do you see out of the window?
    We can see the Headmistress kissing the caretaker.
    Never mind that. The point is . . .

Imagine an object lesson on an elephant, or perhaps on a person you know.

Mixing fact and opinion

Write a lesson based on the Henry VIII sample, where fact and opinion are mixed.

FOR EXAMPLE you could use answers to these questions,
Who is the Prime Minister? Where does he/she live? What is his/her shape? What is his/her job? What is his/her character?

A letter

Write a letter of complaint from a parent of one of the students mentioned in the extracts. The complaint could be about the types of lesson or the treatment of the children.

Exchange letters with your neighbour and write a suitable reply.

Build up a report. Schools ancient and modern

Compare this picture called *A drawing lesson* with an art lesson today.

EDUCATION TODAY

You should each select one or more of these titles to write about as a class project. Compile the pieces of writing to provide your own record of school at the end of the twentieth century. Make this exercise a practice for preparing your coursework folder.

1 My earliest memories of primary school.
2 How I learnt to read and write.
3 School dinners.
4 A lesson I particularly enjoyed.
5 A lesson I particularly disliked.
6 An occasion when I was punished.
7 Teachers I remember.
8 The subjects I like and the subjects I dislike.
9 Discipline in schools today.
10 Is homework an important part of education?
11 Are examinations a good preparation for life?

Presentation is important, as is legible handwriting. Ask other people to read your piece and to comment on your handwriting and presentation.

The facts

Write down the details of one school day, lesson by lesson. Include what you were told, what you wrote, what you did and what you felt.

Decide how your day compared with one from a hundred years ago. Is learning facts still a large part of lessons? Are there more opportunities for you to work by yourself, discuss and say what you feel?

Discussion

A hundred years ago, there were no external examinations, except for those few children who attended private schools, and children left school at 13.
    Work in groups of four.

1 Two play the role of parents of a sixteen-year-old in the 1890s, who left school three years ago and works in a factory.
    The other two are parents of a sixteen-year-old today preparing for examinations.
2 Each pair prepares arguments in favour of leaving school at 13 and 16 respectively.
3 The pairs meet and defend their point of view.
4 At the end of the discussion, each group of four presents its conclusions to the rest of the class.

Writing

Discuss and list the changes which have taken place in education during your lifetime – introduction of computers, less sexism in subject choice, and introduction of new subjects such as electronics.
Write an account of the changes which you think will occur by the year 2000.
Present a timetable for a student of your age in that year.

▭▷ *LANGUAGE PRACTICE*

Using commas

To some extent, commas are a matter of personal opinion. The best advice is to use commas at points where you think it will help your reader to understand what you are writing. Here are five ways of using commas to help make the meaning clear.

1 To separate items in a list.
He picked up the bottle, poured a drink, sat back in the armchair and laughed.
I'd like six oranges, two pounds of apples and a grapefruit.

2 To separate a subordinate (less important) part of a sentence.
When he first visited London, he was disappointed by the noise and the dirt.
She always, if she could manage it, went on holiday to Spain.

3 To separate asides such as *however, by the way, nevertheless* and *therefore.*
He could not, however, open the box.

4 To mark off the names of people who are being addressed.
'Are you listening, Paul?'

5 In the marking of direct speech (see also pages 215–216, Skills reference section).
'I don't know,' said the teacher, 'if that is possible.'

6 Where there is a pause in the sentence, often making a slight change in the content.
'Although I can see what you mean, I do not agree with you.'
'Unless you arrive before two o'clock, there will be no meal for you.'

Test your understanding of commas

Look back at the extracts from *Hard Times* and *The History of Mr Polly* (pages 61–62). Note every example of the comma and say which of the six usages it belongs to.

In this poem the poet James Michie imagines Dooley, a man with a criminal record, being tried for refusing to fight for his country in a war against its enemies.

Dooley is a Traitor

1   'So then you won't fight?'
   'Yes, your Honour,' I said, 'that's right.'
   'Now is it that you simply aren't willing,
   Or have you a fundamental moral objection to killing?'
5   Says the judge, blowing his nose
   And making his words stand to attention in long rows.
   I stand to attention too, but with half a grin
   (In my time I've done a good many in).
   'No objection at all, sir,' I said.
10   'There's a deal of the world I'd rather see dead –
   Such as Johnny Stubbs or Fred Settle or my last
      landlord, Mr Syme.
   Give me a gun and your blessing, your Honour,
      and I'll be killing them all the time.
15   But my conscience says a clear no
   To killing a crowd of gentlemen I don't know.
   Why, I'd as soon think of killing a worshipful judge,
   High-court, like yourself (against whom, God
      knows, I've got no grudge –
20   So far), as murder a heap of foreign folk.
   If you've got no grudge, you've got no joke
   To laugh at after.'
                Now the words never come flowing
   Proper for me till I get the old pipe going.
25   And just as I was poking
   Down baccy, the judge looks up sharp with 'No smoking,
   Mr Dooley. We're not fighting this war for fun.
   And we want a clearer reason why you refuse to
      carry a gun.
30   This war is not a personal feud, it's a fight
   Against wrong ideas on behalf of the Right.
   Mr Dooley, won't you help to destroy evil ideas?'
   'Ah, your Honour, here's
   The tragedy,' I said. 'I'm not a man of the mind.
35   I couldn't find it in my heart to be unkind
   To an idea. I wouldn't know one if I saw one. I
      haven't one of my own.

So I'd best be leaving other people's alone.'
'Indeed,' he sneers at me, 'this defence is
40 Curious for someone with convictions in two senses.
A criminal invokes conscience to his aid
To support an individual withdrawal from a communal
    crusade
Sanctioned by God, led by the Church, against a
45   godless, churchless nation!'
I asked his Honour for a translation.
'You talk of conscience,' he said. 'What do you know
    of the Christian Creed?'
'Nothing, sir, except what I can read.
50 That's the most you can hope for from us jail-birds.
I just open the book here and there and look at the
    words.
And I find when the Lord himself misliked an evil notion
He turned it into a pig and drove it squealing over a
55   cliff into the ocean,
And the loony ran away
And lived to think another day.
There was a clean job done and no blood shed!
Everybody happy and forty wicked thoughts
60   drowned dead.
A neat and Christian murder. None of your mad
    slaughter
Throwing away the brain with the blood and the
    baby with the bathwater.
65 Now I look at the war as a sportsman. It's a matter
    of choosing
The decentest way of losing.
Heads or tails, losers or winners,
We all lose, we're all damned sinners.
70 And I'd rather be with the poor cold people at the
    wall that's shot
Than the bloody guilty devils in the firing-line, in
    Hell and keeping hot.'
'But what right, Dooley, what right,' he cried,
75 'Have you to say the Lord is on your side?'
'That's a dirty crooked question,' back I roared.
'I said not the Lord was on my side, but I was on the
    side of the Lord.'
Then he was up at me and shouting,
80 But by and by he calms: 'Now we're not doubting
Your sincerity, Dooley, only your arguments,
Which don't make sense.'
('Hullo,' I thought, 'that's the wrong way round.
I may be skylarking a bit, but my brainpan's sound.')

85   Then biting his nail and sugaring his words sweet:
      'Keep your head, Mr Dooley. Religion is clearly not
        up your street.
      But let me ask you as a plain patriotic fellow
      Whether you'd stand there so smug and yellow

90   If the foe were attacking your own dear sister.'
      'I'd knock their brains out, mister,
      On the floor,' I said. 'There,' he says kindly, 'I knew
        you were no pacifist.
      It's your straight duty as a man to enlist.

95   The enemy is at the door.' You could have downed
      Me with a feather. 'Where?' I gasp, looking round.
      'Not this door,' he says angered. 'Don't play the clown.
      But they're two thousand miles away planning to
        do us down.

100 Why, the news is full of the deeds of those murderers
        and rapers.'
      'Your Eminence,' I said, 'my father told me never to
        believe the papers
      But to go by my eyes,

105 And at two thousand miles the poor things can't
        tell truth from lies.'
      His fearful spectacles glittered like the moon: 'For
        the last time what right
      Has a man like you to refuse to fight?'

110 'More right,' I said, 'than you.
      You've never murdered a man, so you don't know
        what it is I won't do.
      I've done it in good hot blood, so haven't I the right
        to make bold

115 To declare that I shan't do it in cold?'
      Then the judge rises in a great rage
      And writes *Dooley is a Traitor* in black upon a page
      And tells me I must die.
      'What, me?' says I.

120 'If you still won't fight.'
      'Well, yes, your Honour,' I said, 'that's right.'

                             James Michie

Understanding – following an argument

1 Using your own words as far as possible give Dooley's answers to each of these questions from the judge.

'Have you a moral objection to killing?'   (Answer in 30–40 words)
'Won't you help to destroy evil ideas?'   (Answer in 20–30 words)
'What do you know of the Christian Creed?'   (Answer in 20–30 words)
'What right have you to say the Lord is on your side?'   (Answer in 10–15 words)
'For the last time, what right has a man like you to refuse to fight?'   (Answer in 20–30 words)

2 In a passage of 20–30 words say what overall point the poet is making about war.

Directed writing

In 25–30 lines, either in prose or play form, outline an argument you had with someone.
Represent the other person's view fairly, and avoid simple contradictions (Yes, it is/No, it isn't).

4 Describing people

You are asked to

→ Discuss a 'Wanted' notice

→ Compare two character portraits

→ Write a similar portrait of someone you know

→ Analyse the differing methods through which a character is created

→ Understand the relationship between character and plot

→ Write a passage illustrating character in action

→ Criticise other attempts at the same exercise

Examination practice – answer questions on an autobiographical poem

FIFTY POUNDS REWARD
for the arrest of

JOHN HATFIELD

IMPOSTER, SWINDLER, THIEF

who lately married a young woman called

THE BEAUTY OF BUTTERMERE
under an assumed name.

His height is five feet, 10 inches, age about 44, with a thick nose, long fair hair, a scar near his chin, rather fat and limps on his left leg. The two middle fingers of his left hand are stiff from an old wound.

He speaks very fast with an Irish accent. He is very fond of young ladies; he often talks of his adventures in the war and his wounds; he talks about his estates in Derbyshire and traces his family tree back to Edward IV. He boasts about duels he has been in and of his travels in Egypt and Italy. These are all shameful lies, but he has a charming manner and has tricked many innocent people.

He was in Scarborough Gaol for seven years. Then he married a lady in Devon and deserted her and his two children. He then craftily got himself made a partner with respectable merchants in Dorset and swindled them out of a large sum of money.

He pretends he is very religious and makes a point of going to church and listening to preachers.

On September 9th he married a respectable young woman near Lake Buttermere. He called himself the Honourable Colonel Hope and the unlucky lady was tricked. He has made off with much of her money and jewels.

On 25th October he was seen at Ravenglass, in Cumberland, wrapped in a large sailor's coat and with a beard to disguise himself. He might be hiding in Liverpool or some nearby port, waiting to leave the country.

Whoever will arrest him and give information to Mr. Taunton, no.4, Pump Court, Temple, so that he may be put in one of His Majesty's gaols, will receive

FIFTY POUNDS REWARD

November 5th, 1802 (P. Stuart, Daily Advertiser Office 33, Fleet Street)

A 'Wanted' notice

The purpose of the description of John Hatfield is identification. It contains all the points you associate with description.

> appearance
> dress
> habits
> typical actions
> likes and dislikes

But although John Hatfield sounds an interesting villain, there is no life to the description. There is no relationship between the writer and the portrait; no real feelings are involved.

Writing

Bringing John Hatfield to life

Imagine that you recognise John Hatfield. You ask if he is John Hatfield. Write 20 lines of conversation. Remember he will be trickily evasive.

Understanding – *On a Portrait of a Deaf Man*

Read the poem on the next page.

1 Write down the appropriate details from the portrait for each of these: appearance, dress, habits, typical actions, likes and dislikes.
2 What does the poet remember as soon as he thinks about his father's appearance?
3 What expressions does the poet use to show how horrible these thoughts are?
4 How does he link the details of the father in life with the father dead?
5 What sign of bitterness is there in the last verse?
6 In verses 2, 4 and 7, how is the form of the verse used to contrast the living and the dead father?

Describing people

In this poem it is the feelings, rather than the details, which bring the portrait to life.

On a Portrait of a Deaf Man

The kind old face, the egg-shaped head,
   The tie, discreetly loud,
The loosely fitted shooting clothes,
   A closely fitting shroud.

He liked old City dining-rooms,
   Potatoes in their skin,
But now his mouth is wide to let
   The London clay come in.

He took me on long silent walks
   In country lanes when young,
He knew the name of ev'ry bird
   But not the song it sung.

And when he could not hear me speak
   He smiled and looked so wise
That now I do not like to think
   Of maggots in his eyes.

He liked the rain-washed Cornish air
   And smell of ploughed-up soil,
He liked a landscape big and bare
   And painted it in oil.

But least of all he liked that place
   Which hangs on Highgate Hill
Of soaked Carrara-covered earth
   For Londoners to fill.

He would have liked to say good-bye,
   Shake hands with many friends,
In Highgate now his finger-bones
   Stick through his finger-ends.

You, God, who treat him thus and thus,
   Say 'Save his soul and pray.'
You ask me to believe You and
   I only see decay.

John Betjeman

The Ratcatcher

1   In the afternoon the ratcatcher came to the filling station. He came sidling up
the driveway with a stealthy, soft-treading gait, making no noise at all with his
feet on the gravel. He had an army knapsack slung over one shoulder and he
was wearing an old-fashioned black jacket with large pockets. His brown
5   corduroy trousers were tied around the knees with pieces of white string.
　　'Yes?' Claud asked, knowing very well who he was.
　　'Rodent operative.' His small dark eyes moved swiftly over the premises.
　　'The ratcatcher?'
　　'That's me.'
10　　The man was lean and brown with a sharp face and two long sulphur-
coloured teeth that protruded from the upper jaw, overlapping the lower lip,
pressing it inward. The ears were thin and pointed and set far back on the
head, near the nape of the neck. The eyes were almost black, but when they
looked at you there was a flash of yellow somewhere inside them.

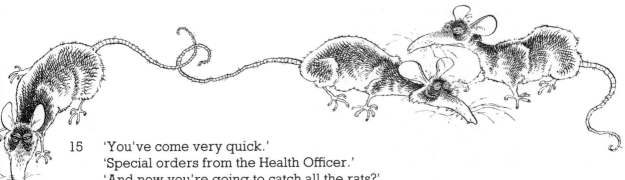

15　　'You've come very quick.'
　　'Special orders from the Health Officer.'
　　'And now you're going to catch all the rats?'
　　'Yep.'
　　The kind of dark furtive eyes he had were those of an animal that lives
20　its life peering out cautiously and forever from a hole in the ground.
　　'How are you going to catch 'em?'
　　'Ah-h-h,' the ratman said darkly. 'That's all accordin' to where they is.'
　　'Trap 'em, I suppose.'

　　'Trap 'em!' he cried, disgusted. 'You won't catch many rats that way! Rats
25　isn't rabbits, you know.'
　　He held his face up high, sniffing the air with a nose that twitched
perceptibly from side to side.
　　'No,' he said, scornfully. 'Trappin's no way to catch a rat. Rats is clever, let
me tell you that. If you want to catch 'em, you got to know 'em. You got to
30　know rats on this job.'

I could see Claud staring at him with a certain fascination.

'They're more clever'n dogs, rats is.'

'Get away.'

'You know what they do? They watch you! All the time you're goin' round
35 preparin' to catch 'em, they're sittin' quietly in dark places, watchin' you.' The
man crouched, stretching his stringy neck far forward.

'So what do you do?' Claud asked.

'Ah! That's it, you see. That's where you got to know rats.'

'How d'you catch 'em?'

40 'There's ways,' the ratman said, leering. 'There's various ways.'

He paused, nodding his repulsive head sagely up and down. 'It's all
dependin',' he said, 'on where they is. This ain't a sewer job, is it?'

'No, it's not a sewer job.'

'Tricky things, sewer jobs. Yes,' he said, delicately sniffing the air to the left
45 of him with his mobile nose-end, 'sewer jobs is very tricky things.'

'Not especially, I shouldn't think.'

'Oh-ho. You shouldn't, shouldn't you! Well, I'd like to see *you* do a sewer
job! Just exactly how would *you* set about it, I'd like to know?'

'Nothing to it. I'd just poison 'em, that's all.'

50 'And where exactly would you put the poison, might I ask?'

'Down the sewer. Where the hell you think I put it!'

'There!' the ratman cried, triumphant. 'I knew it! Down the sewer! And you
know what'd happen then? Get washed away, that's all. Sewer's like a river,
y'know.'

55 'That's what *you* say,' Claud answered. 'That's only what *you* say.'

'It's facts.'

'All right, then, all right. So what would *you* do, Mr Know-all?'

'That's exactly where you got to know rats, on a sewer job.'

'Come on then, let's have it.'

60 'Now listen. I'll tell you.' The ratman advanced a step closer, his voice
became secretive and confidential, the voice of a man divulging fabulous
professional secrets. 'You works on the understandin' that a rat is a gnawin'
animal, see. Rats *gnaws*. Anythin' you give 'em, don't matter what it is, anythin'
new they never seen before, and what do they do? They *gnaws* it. So now!

65 There you are! You get a sewer job on your hands. And what d'you do?'

His voice had the soft throaty sound of a croaking frog and he seemed to

speak all his words with an immense wet-lipped relish, as though they tasted
good on the tongue. The accent was similar to Claud's, the broad soft accent of
the Buckinghamshire countryside, but his voice was more throaty, the words
70 more fruity in his mouth.

'All you do is you go down the sewer and you take along some ordinary
paper bags, just ordinary brown paper bags, and these bags is filled with
plaster of Paris powder. Nothin' else. Then you suspend the bags from the
roof of the sewer so they hang down not quite touchin' the water. See? Not
75 quite touchin', and just high enough so a rat can reach 'em.'
  Claud was listening, rapt.
  'There you are, y'see. Old rat comes swimmin' along the sewer and sees the
bag. He stops. He takes a sniff at it and it don't smell so bad anyway. So what's
he do then?'
80   'He *gnaws* it,' Claud cried, delighted.
  'There! That's it! That's exactly it! He starts *gnawin'* away at the bag and the
bag breaks and the old rat gets a mouthful of powder for his pains.'
  'Well?'
  'That does him.'
85   'What? Kills him?'
  'Yep. Kills him stony!'
  'Plaster of Paris ain't poisonous, you know.'

  'Ah! There you are! That's exackly where you're wrong, see.
This powder swells. When you wet it, it swells. Gets into the rat's
90 tubes and swells right up and kills him quicker'n anythin' in the world.'
  'No!'
  'That's where you got to know rats.'
  The ratman's face glowed with a stealthy pride, and he rubbed his stringy
fingers together, holding the hands up close to the face. Claud watched him,
95 fascinated.
  'Now – where's them rats?' The word 'rats' came out of his mouth soft and
throaty, with a rich fruity relish as though he were gargling with melted
butter. 'Let's take a look at them *rraats*.'
  'Over there in the hayrick across the road.'
100   'Not in the house?' he asked, obviously disappointed.
  'No. Only around the hayrick. Nowhere else.'

'I'll wager they're in the house too. Like as not gettin' in all your food in the night and spreadin' disease and sickness. You got any disease here?' he asked, looking first at me, then at Claud.

105 'Everyone fine here.'

'Quite sure?'

'Oh yes.'

'You never know, you see. You could be sickenin' for it weeks and weeks and not feel it. Then all of a sudden – bang! – and it's got you. That's why Dr
110 Arbuthnot's so particular. That's why he sent me out so quick, see. To stop the spreadin' of disease.'

He had now taken upon himself the mantle of the Health Officer. A most important rat he was now, deeply disappointed that we were not suffering from bubonic plague.

115 'I feel fine,' Claud said, nervously.

The ratman searched his face again, but said nothing.

'And how are you goin' to catch 'em in the hayrick?'

The ratman grinned, a crafty toothy grin. He reached down into his knapsack and withdrew a large tin which he held up level with his face. He
120 peered around one side of it at Claud.

'Poison!' he whispered. But he pronounced it *pye-zn*, making it into a soft, dark, dangerous word. 'Deadly *pye-zn*, that's what this is!' He was weighing the tin up and down in his hands as he spoke. 'Enough here to kill a million men!'

125 'Terrifying,' Claud said.

'Exackly it! They'd put you inside for six months if they caught you with even a spoonful of this,' he said, wetting his lips with his tongue. He had a habit of craning his head forward on his neck as he spoke.

'Want to see?' he asked, taking a penny from his pocket, prising open the
130 lid. 'There now! There it is!' He spoke fondly, almost lovingly of the stuff, and he held it forward for Claud to look.

'Corn? Or barley is it?'

'It's oats. Soaked in deadly *pye-zn*. You take just one of them grains in your mouth and you'd be a gonner in five minutes.'

135 'Honest?'

'Yep. Never out of me sight, this tin.'

He caressed it with his hands and gave it a little shake so that the oat grains rustled softly inside.

'But not today. Your rats don't get this today. They wouldn't have it anyway.
140 That they wouldn't. There's where you got to know rats. Rats is suspicious. Terrible suspicious, rats is. So today they gets some nice clean tasty oats as'll do 'em no harm in the world. Fatten 'em, that's all it'll do. And tomorrow they gets the same again. And it'll taste so good there'll be all the rats in the districk comin' along after a couple of days.'

145 'Rather clever.'

'You got to be clever on this job. You got to be cleverer'n a rat and that's sayin' something.'

'You've almost got to be a rat yourself,' I said. It slipped out in error, before I had time to stop myself, and I couldn't really help it because I was looking at 150 the man at the time. But the effect upon him was surprising.

'There!' he cried. 'Now you got it! Now you really said something! A good ratter's got to be more like a rat than anythin' else in the world! Cleverer even than a rat, and that's not an easy thing to be, let me tell you!'

Roald Dahl

Characteristics of the ratcatcher

Write down the most distinctive and memorable details about the ratcatcher for each of these headings.

1 Face
2 Type of walk
3 Clothes
4 Accent
5 Manner of speech. Choose one example to show *how* he speaks, whether it is for instance in a boastful, modest, friendly, or hostile way.
6 Voice. Choose an example that illustrates the *sound* of his voice.
7 Habits. Choose one movement that is typical of him.

The ratcatcher in the story

Dahl does not present the details about his character in the same way as Betjeman does. You learn about them *as the ratcatcher does his job and tells us about it*. His feelings about his job are the most important part of the description.

1 How do the ratcatcher's first words show his pride in his job?
2 How does his method of conversation show that he is anxious to show his skill?
3 What shows that he is contemptuous of the lay person's knowledge of ratcatching?
4 What indications are there that the ratcatcher admires rats?
5 When the author implies that the ratcatcher is rather like a rat, what is surprising about his reaction? What does the reaction show?

How the author uses Claud

In a paragraph of 50–60 words illustrate how the author uses Claud to show that the ratcatcher is repulsive and annoying but fascinating.

Writing

1 Write a story about a person who, like the ratcatcher, has animal characteristics, for instance someone who looks and moves like a cat and who likes warm fires and attention but is sly and solitary.

2 Describe a meeting you have had with someone who made a strong impression on you. He or she may be either fascinating or unpleasant or even both, like the ratcatcher.

    Build up an impression of the person by including different types of detail, without giving the appearance of a list. Include your feelings during the meeting (they may change) or use a third person, similar to Claud, to show the effect the person has on others.

NOTE

The pieces that follow on the next three pages are answers to this writing task. Use them either as preparation for your own work or as comparison pieces after you have finished.

▷ *LANGUAGE PRACTICE*

Compare three pieces of writing

These three pieces all relate encounters with an unpleasant person. They were all written in controlled conditions – a thirty-five-minute lesson.

Each piece has been marked and commented on. Do you agree with the comments? Spelling and punctuation errors have been indicated by a circle. Correct each one.

An encounter with an unpleasant person

I still remember vividly one afternoon when I was approached by a man in his car. I was ten years old and with my friend Catherine. We had just come out of the post office and were walking along the High Street in Fenstanton to my house, when a car drew up next to us. A man leaned out of the window and shouted 'Hello'. I smiled and began to walk away when he shouted at us again. 'Come here a minute,' he said. 'I want you to do me a favour.'

Forgetting everything I had been taught about 'not talking to strangers', I walked over to the car. I looked into the car and was horrified at what I saw. The man was wearing nothing but a vest. He told me to put my hand through the window and touch him. I backed away and started to walk quickly along the pavement. The man started his car and drove slowly alongside me. I was terrified. I was unable to run because I was wearing flip-flops and it was hard enough trying to walk in them. We reached the newsagents and ran inside. We didn't tell anyone about the man, but waited a couple of minutes until we were sure that he had gone.

We left the shop and began to walk to my house again when I noticed his car parked outside the Tudor Hotel. We were so scared that we ran all the way to Catherine's house. I remember that I didn't want to go to my house because I was scared of telling my Mum what had happened.

When we reached Catherine's house Catherine told her Mum and Dad what had happened. They told us to show them where his car was parked. When we reached the Tudor carpark his car had gone. We walked down to the post office but there was no sign of his car.

It was left at that. We didn't phone the police because we were unable to give a description of the man or his car. For quite a long time I had nightmares about it. Gradually I began to forget the man and what had happened. I often wonder now if it was all just a dream. But I can remember it too well for it to have been a dream. I never did tell my Mum. I don't know why. I think if she ever found out now she would be hurt that I didn't tell her. I realise how lucky I was when I hear the terrible stories about abducted children. If I had gone with the man in his car I might never have been seen again.

Good use of short sentences

Notice how you have been able to make the man seem unpleasant because of your feelings without any detailed description

15/20 *Fluently written. Good detail. You write with more conviction than usual because of the strong impression the unpleasantness of the incident made on you.*

An encounter with an unpleasant person

A small boy came into our History class.
'Would Sharon Jackson go to see Miss Andrews,' he said.
As I reached for my blazer a cold shiver ran up and down my spine.
What had I done? What had I said?
As I walked down the corridor my legs felt like jelly. I turned the corner
and my eyes focussed on the block letters.
'Miss Andrews. Year Tutor'
I knocked and Miss Andrews opened the door, her blue eyes full of evil.
'Ah yes, Sharon. Come with me.'
She rushed off down the corridor. I followed, my eyes fixed on the little
hole in her tights. She opened the door of Room 8 and said in a squeaky,
sarcastic voice, 'After you, Miss Jackson.'
My eyes filled with horror and my face flushed like a beetroot. She was
putting me in a first year class.
'Sit at the back, Sharon,' she said and smiled a sarcastic smile.
Her teeth were crooked and cracked. (✳)
I walked to the back. I was trembling like a leaf with rage. All the
small kids stared at me.
Then she started the lesson. It was Latin. I'd never done Latin. I
sat there staring at the desk.
'Perhaps Sharon could tell us,' she suddenly said.
'Tell you what, Miss?' I mumbled.
'The answer of course.'
I hadn't been listening. I didn't know what they were talking about.
'No, I can't,' I said.
'Oh dear,' she sighed. 'And you such a big girl.'
All the kids looked at me again.
For the rest of the lesson I sat thinking of things I'd like to do to
Miss Andrews. I'd drop her down a well, for instance. When she was
struggling to escape I'd shout ◯
'Can't you get out, Miss? And you such a very big girl.'
My daydreaming was interrupted ◯
'Sharon, wait behind please,' said a nagging voice.
My stomach started to turn to ice and my palms were sweating.
'First I'll have your rings, bangles and necklace.'
I took them off and handed them to her. I wished I dared say
she'd look like mutton dressed as lamb in them. Move like this
'Thank-you,' she said, making the words sound like a cash register.
'Now,' said Miss Andrews. 'Chemistry - Mr Caunt - no homework -
much cheek.'
I never thought he'd report me. There were plenty of others messing about.
'Anything to declare for the defence?' she said sarcastically.
'No,' I said.
'No what?'
'No, Miss.'
'One more complaint about you and you'll join a first-year class
permanently,' she said.
I walked down the corridor feeling sick and faint. Tears started to well
up in my eyes. I was crying through the shame of letting her humiliate me.
'Old cow. Old skinny cow. Thieving old cow,' I kept muttering as I
returned to my lesson.

14/20 Good. You have made the person sound most unpleasant and spiteful, particularly
in the dialogue. A redraft, leaving out the clichés, and including a few
more details (for instance, about the first years' reactions to you) would improve
the piece.

[left margin annotations:]
Good dramatic start, but spoiled by you expressing your own feelings in clichés.

Good word

Again, clichés. We would guess your feelings about being put into a first year class, anyway.

(✳) Good detail; perhaps you could express your feelings as you are giving more details:
'I hated her crooked and cracked teeth, the hole in her tights,' and ...

[right margin annotations:]
Good use of short sentences

You have caught the sarcasm well.

Good - much better way of expressing feelings

Here you go again!

More like this

Very good simile

82

An encounter with an unpleasant person

There was a shuffle of feet, and from the shadows emerged the dirty hunched figure of a wino. From a distance all I could see was his stained raincoat hanging losely on his bony sholders and his battered trilby balancing precareosly above it. Disapearing into another shadow he discarded an empty brown glass bottel with a casual toss over the sholder. The bottel fell and smashed. My attention was drawn away from the shattered glass fragments by the clatter of mettal dustbins and the breaking of more glass. A long silent pause followed and I decided that I should investigate.

He lay there in a huge heap of rubbish with his head pressed awkwardly against the wall. I kicked his shoe to see if he was concous and with one quick movement he sprang up and grabbed me by the collar.

'Where's your cash, son?' he said in a rough voice. The smell of his breath was overpowering. Five minutes talking to him and you would be as drunk as he was. I said nothing as his tight grip constricted my windpipe. ✳

Still holding me by the colar he rifeled through my pockets with his other hand. Finding nothing he swung me round and pushed me against the wall. Due to the street light over the wall I could see all of his face. He was unshaven with raging ackne making his face look like a hedgehog with chicken pox. Two bloodshot eyes glared out from under the brim of his hat. He then repeated his request for money This time more impaciently.

'I, I, haven't got any, I'm skint,' I stuttered. He eased his grip and looked disapointed.

'Sorry Mate, I'm a failure.' To my surprise he released me. I stepped back and he sank to the floor with his face in his hands.

I turned and ran without looking back.

Discussion – do appearances tell?

Discuss the type of person each of these is. They have something in common.
(Turn to page 86 for the answer.)

A

B

C

D

━━━ ▥▷ *EXAMINATION PRACTICE*

Read this poem.

Autobiographical Note

1   Beeston, the place, near Nottingham;
      We lived there for three years or so.
      Each Saturday at two o'clock
      We queued up for the matinée,
5   All the kids for streets around
      With snotty noses, giant caps,
      Cut down coats and heavy boots,
      The natural enemies of cops
      And schoolteachers. Profane and hoarse
10   We scrambled, yelled and fought until
      The Picture Palace opened up
      And then, like Hamelin children, forced
      Our bony way into the Hall.
      That much is easy to recall;
15   Also the reek of chewing-gum,
      Gob-stoppers and liquorice,
      But of the flickering myths themselves
      Not much remains. The hero was
      A milky, wide-brimmed hat, a shape
20   Astride the arched white stallion.
      The villain's horse and hat were black.
      Disbelief did not exist
      And laundered virtue always won
      With quicker gun and harder fist
25   And all of us applauded it.
      Yet I remember moments when
      In solitude I'd find myself
      Brooding on the sooty man,
      The bristling villain, who could move
30   Imagination in a way
      The well-shaved hero never could,
      And even warm the nervous heart
      With something oddly close to love.

                    Vernon Scannell

Understanding and directed writing

1 Today there is much debate about poverty, particularly in cities, and unruly behaviour by children. In a passage of about 60 words say what evidence there is of poverty and unruly behaviour in the Beeston of the poet's youth.

2 Choose *two* of the following phrases and say what you think the poet means by them.

   a) 'like Hamelin children'
   b) 'laundered virtue'
   c) 'flickering myths'

3 What point do you think the poet is making in the last eight lines ('Yet I remember . . . close to love')?

4 *Either*
   a) Briefly describe an occasion when you have shared the poet's feelings for a 'villain'.
   or
   b) Say why you think that the villain of books, films or plays should always receive his or her just deserts.

5 Do you think the form of the poem suits the title? (Refer particularly to the first two lines.)

6 Write a poem about poverty or unruly behaviour which you have seen or experienced. Vernon Scannell achieves great detail with few words. Try to imitate this quality.

The characters on page 84 are all murderers.

A *Harry Thaw* – rich, spoilt, cruel. Murdered Stanford White, famous architect, June 1906.

B *Florence Maybrick* – poisoned her husband. Bought a large quantity of flypaper and soaked it in water to obtain arsenic.

C *Johnny Torrio* – gangster. A talent for organising murder and violence.

D *John Wilkes Booth* – murdered President Lincoln.

5 A tale to tell

Recounting experience

You are asked to

⟶ **Distinguish between fact and emotion**

⟶ **Discuss the nature and cause of prejudice**

⟶ **Recount an experience that changed your views**

⟶ **Criticise a pupil's writing on the same subject**

⟶ **Study the importance of stress in speech**

Examination practice – answer questions on a poem

Cathy's Story

1 I'm taking part in what seems like a bad film. There's me, holed up in the
bank; I'm about to step outside with my sawn-off shotgun, and waiting for me
are hundreds of huge cops, armed and very hostile. Actually, I haven't a sawn-
off shotgun, only a home-made placard that says, 'No imprisonment without
5 trial.' I lied about the bank too. I'm in the offices of Black Sash, an organisation
that explains to South African black people their legal rights – very few! I'm
not even alone; there are about thirty of us, and we're planning to display our
banners on the streets of Johannesburg.

*The picture shows Cathy Urwin at a football match in Soweto, during her stay in South
Africa.*

But what I certainly didn't lie about are the police. They've been gathering
10 all day; they've got wind of the dreadful thing we are about to do.

I'm going with Jackie in her car. Two black boys have just asked for a lift to
their demonstration points. Of course, we can't all demonstrate together. Even
two of us standing together would constitute an 'unlawful assembly' and
certain imprisonment, so we plan to stand singly at street corners.
15   The boys are ready; so am I. Jackie is still busy trying to fold her banner, so
that it can't be read as we move to her car.
I look through the window. There's a cop about every five yards. I fight
down an urge to giggle. Well, it has its funny side. Half the Johannesburg
police force lined up to get us for daring to suggest that if they lock people up
20 would they please have a reason – other than that they don't like their black
looks.

They cannot be serious! But they look very serious, even sinister –
enormous, somehow shapeless men in light blue uniforms and dark glasses.
I have to remind myself that they believe in a system where a fifth of the
25 population owns ninety per cent of the land, where there's one doctor for
every 400 whites and one for every 44,000 blacks, where every black person
carries a pass by which the whites control where he lives, works, travels,
where the law forbids a black person to have a skilled job, where . . .
They can be serious. If they believe their system's right, they can believe
30 my placard's as dangerous as a sawn-off shotgun.

'Ready,' says Jackie, and we plunge into the street, feeling a bit like Butch
Cassidy and Sundance rushing out of their shelter to be mown down by half
the Spanish army.
But the cops don't shoot us. We make for the car, jostled and poked by white
35 passers-by. They don't jeer, but in their faces are contempt, hate and,
perhaps, fear. Maybe I'm just hoping the fear. Perhaps it's just righteous shock
at the disgusting sight – two white girls with two blacks, carrying placards
with outrageous words on them.
We're into the car and away, placards tucked safely under the seats. But as
40 we move off two cars full of cops slide out of the side-streets. A third joins
them.
'They're following us – three cars full,' I say. Jackie nods and looks nervous,
as she weaves in and out of parked cars and pedestrians.

I still can't quite believe we're not taking part in a Pink Panther film and that
45 Clouseau won't suddenly appear on the roof of our car holding a huge black
ball with BOMB chalked on it. To add to the air of unreality the huge cops are
all squashed in tiny cars, like elephants in telephone boxes.
Now they're gaining on us, the lead car almost on our bumper.
'Are they just trying to scare us?' I ask.
50   The others say nothing; they're more experienced than I. They know there's

nothing very comic about the South African police.

'It's not good. Better not risk dropping you,' Jackie says to the two black boys.

They nod agreement.

55 'We'll take you back to Black Sash. They'd arrest you here before you got your feet to the pavement.'

Another twenty minutes of chase round the streets of Johannesburg and we're back where we started from. We drop our passengers and then set off south, heading for the university, where Jackie's husband works.

60 'We'll park as near as we can, and make a run for it,' says Jackie.

'But we haven't even done anything; we haven't even held up our placards.'

Jackie just pointed to the words on my placard.

'Remember what we're protesting about.'

Now we're out of the city centre. Two cars have dropped away. We speed
65 up; so does the remaining car. We hit the ramp of the multi-storey entrance far too fast, but just manage to stop before the wooden barrier. I grab the ticket. We shoot off just as the cop car grinds to a halt behind us. Now it's a lunatic chase round the hairpin corners of the multi-storey. Up we go, six, seven, eight floors. Suddenly we're out into the sunshine of the roof. Plenty of
70 room to park – even sideways, as Jackie has done.

She grabs the keys. We're out of the car in two seconds and running down the ramp that connects the car park to the University campus. The cops must have slowed. We still hear them grinding up the floors.

'Is it sanctuary in here?' I gasp.

75 'No, but if we hide here there's a chance they won't bother looking for us.'

They don't. In fact from a window inside we watch them. They've parked next to Jackie's car. Now they've clambered outside – only three of them. They stretch their legs and begin to peer at the car. One wrenches open the door, pulls out the placards and transfers them to the cop car. Another takes
80 hold of a windscreen wiper. Slowly and deliberately he twists it until it breaks. He drops it on the bonnet, and then twists off the other. His two friends seem to be studying the wheels.

'What are the bastards doing?' I ask, and am slightly shocked. In the six weeks I'd been in South Africa I'd been determined to keep my dislike of the
85 white South Africans under wraps – I'd been determined to look at it from 'the other side'. Now I suddenly conclude there isn't another side. There is only one side to be on – and it isn't the side of those huge nasty sods who, it is now clear, are letting our tyres down.

A few well-aimed kicks at the bodywork and they are gone.

90 Jackie is shaking a little; so am I. The fear somehow gets you after the event. We wait two hours before borrowing a foot-pump.

Next day I'm back on normal duty in the Black Sash offices, vainly trying to give advice about exorbitant gas bills and comfort for people sacked at a month's notice. I can't get used to it. Why do elderly black people approach

95 me as hesitantly as if I were a queen? I know why really, of course. I had just a taste of why yesterday. Of course my experience compared to theirs is the difference between a blind man and one who has just shut his eyes for a moment.

    I know I can escape by just opening my eyes – a white girl with a British
100 passport can't really understand apartheid. Nevertheless, although yesterday's demonstration was a failure – not one placard was actually displayed – it was in one sense a success for me. I now know for certain that there's not two sides to every question.

based on an interview with Cathy Urwin

Thinking about the story

The facts

Cathy says:

> In the six weeks I'd been in South Africa I'd been determined to keep my dislike of white South Africans under wraps – I'd been determined to look at it from 'the other side'.

Cathy obviously had strong feelings about South Africa before she went. Perhaps these feelings biased her, despite her determination not to prejudge.

Write a factual report that Cathy might make as a protest to the South African authorities about the incident. Exclude her impressions and feelings.

The feelings

Cathy's fellow demonstrators are more experienced:
    They know there's nothing very comic about the South African police.

In a paragraph of 100–150 words show how Cathy's mood changes from finding the situation comic and silly to feeling fear and anger. Include both the changing feelings and the language used to express them.

The causes

Cathy finds the situation comic at first because she is still looking at it from her experience of a different political and legal system. She knew the system and laws of South Africa, but had not experienced their consequences. In a paragraph of about 100 words say what you discover from the story about the system and laws in South Africa.

Discussion

What does Cathy mean by her conclusion? Is it justified?
    In all societies there is prejudice. What is basically different about South African prejudice against blacks and colour prejudice in other countries?

Use this passage to widen the discussion. It is an extract from *The Baker's Story* by V S Naipaul.

The Baker's Story

The baker, Youngman, began baking bread for a Chinese bread shop. His bread was very popular, so when the Chinese owners died, he borrowed money and opened a bread shop of his own.

1 Now the funny thing happen. In Laventille the people couldn't have enough of the bread I was baking – and in the last few months was me was doing the baking. But now trouble. I baking better bread than the people of Arouca ever see, and I can't get one single feller to come in like man through my rickety
5 old front door and buy a penny hops bread. You hear all this talk about quality being its own advertisement? Don't believe it, boy. Is quality plus something else. And I didn't have this something else. I begin to wonder what the hell it could be. I say is because I new in Arouca that this thing happening. But no, I new, I get stale, and the people not flocking in their hundreds to the old shop.
10 Day after day I baking two or three quarts good and all this just remaining and going dry and stale, and the only bread I selling is to the man from the government farm, buying stale cakes and bread for the cows or pigs or whatever they have up there. And was good bread. So I get down on the old knees and I pray as though I want to wear them out. And still I getting the same
15 answer: 'Youngman' – was always the way I uses to get call in these prayers – 'Youngman, you just bake bread.'

Pappa! This was a thing. Interest on the loan piling up every month. Some

months I borrow from aunty and anybody else who kind enough to listen just
to pay off the interest. And things get so low that I uses to have to go out and
20 pretend to people that I was working for another man bakery and that I was
going to bake their dough cheap-cheap. And in Arouca cheap mean cheap.
And the little cash I picking up in this disgraceful way was just about enough to
keep the wolf from the door, I tell you.
    Jeezan. Look at confusion. The old place in Arouca so damn out of the way –
25 was why I did buy it, too, thinking that they didn't have no bakery there and
that they would be glad of the good Grenadian-baked – the place so out of the
way nobody would want to buy it. It ain't even insure or anything, so it can't
get in a little fire accident or anything – not that I went in for that sort of thing.
And every time I go down on my knees, the answer coming straight back at
30 me: 'Youngman, you just bake bread.'

    Well, for the sake of the Lord I baking one or two quarts regular every day,
though I begin to feel that the Lord want to break me, and I begin to feel too
that this was His punishment for what I uses to do to the Chinese people in
their bakery. I was beginning to feel bad and real ignorant. I uses to stay away
35 from the bakery after baking those quarts for the Lord – nothing to lock up,
nothing to thief – and, when any of the Laventille boys drop in on the way to
Manzanilla and Balandra and those other beaches on the Sabbath, I uses to tell
them, making a joke out of it, that I was 'loafing'. They uses to laugh like hell,
too. It have nothing in the whole world so funny as to see a man you know flat
40 out on his arse and catching good hell.

    The Indian feller was getting anxious about his cash, and you couldn't blame
him, either, because some months now he not even seeing his interest. And
this begin to get me down, too. I remember how all the man did ask me when I
went to him for money was: 'You sure you want to bake bread? You feel you
45 have a hand for baking bread?' And yes – yes I tell him, and just like that he
shell out the cash. And now he was getting anxious. So one day, after baking
those loaves for the Lord, I take a Arima Bus Service bus to Port of Spain to see
this feller. I was feeling brave enough on the way. But as soon as I see the old
sea and get a whiff of South Quay and the bus touch the Railway Station
50 terminus my belly start going pweh-pweh. I decide to roam about the city for a
little.

    Was a hot morning, *petit-carême* weather, and in those days a coconut uses
still to cost .04. Well, it had this coconut cart in the old square and I stop by it.
It was a damn funny thing to see. The seller was a black feller. And you
55 wouldn't know how funny this was, unless you know that every coconut seller
in the island is Indian. They have this way of handling a cutlass that black
people don't have. Coconut in left hand; with right hand bam, bam, bam with
cutlass, and coconut cut open, ready to drink. I ain't never see a coconut seller
chop his hand. And here was this black feller doing this bam-bam business on
60 a coconut with a cutlass. It was as funny as seeing a black man wearing dhoti
and turban. The sweetest part of the whole business was that this black feller

was, forgetting looks, just like an Indian. He was talking Hindustani to a lot of
Indian fellers, who was giving him jokes like hell, but he wasn't minding. It
does happen like that sometimes with black fellers who live a lot with Indians
65 in the country. They putting away curry, talking Indian, and behaving just like
Indians. Well, I take a coconut from this black man and then went on to see the
feller about the money.

He was more sad than vex when I tell him, and if I was in his shoes I woulda
be sad, too. Is a hell of a thing when you see your money gone and you ain't
70 getting the sweet little kisses from the interest every month. Anyway, he say
he would give me three more months' grace, but that if I didn't start shelling
out at the agreed rate he would have to foreclose. 'You put me in a hell of a
position,' he say. 'Look at me. You think I want a shop in Arouca?'

I was feeling a little better when I leave the feller, and who I should see
75 when I leave but Percy. Percy was an old rango who uses to go to the
Laventille elementary school with me. I never know a boy get so much cut-
arse as Percy. But he grow up real hard and ignorant with it, and now he
wearing fancy clothes like a saga boy, and talking about various business
offers. I believe he was selling insurance – is a thing that nearly every idler
80 doing in Trinidad, and, mark my words, the day coming when you going to
see those fellers trying to sell insurance to one another. Anyway, Percy
getting on real flash, and he say he want to stand me a lunch for old times'
sake. He makes a few of the usual ignorant Trinidadian jokes about
Grenadians, and we went up to the Angostura Bar. I did never go there
85 before, and wasn't the sort of place you would expect a rango like Percy to be
welcome. But we went up there and Percy start throwing his weight around
with the waiters, and, mind you, they wasn't even a quarter as black as Percy.
Is a wonder they didn't abuse him, especially with all those fair people
around. After the drinks Percy say, 'Where you want to have this lunch?'

90 Me, I don't know a thing about the city restaurants, and when Percy talk
about food all I was expecting was rice and peas or a roti off a Indian stall or a
mauby and rock cake in some parlour. And is a damn hard thing to have
people, even people as ignorant as Percy, showing off on you, especially
when you carrying two nails in your pocket to make the jingling noise. So I tell
95 Percy we could go to a parlour or a bar. But he say, 'No, no. When I treat my
friends, I don't like black people meddling with my food.'

And was only then that the thing hit me. I suppose that what Trinidadians say
about the stupidness of Grenadians have a little truth, though you have to live
in a place for a long time before you get to know it really well. Then the thing
100 hit me, man.

When black people in Trinidad go to a restaurant they don't like to see
black people meddling with their food. And then I see that though Trinidad
have every race and every colour, every race have to do special things. But
look, man. If you want to buy a snowball, who you buying it from? You
105 wouldn't buy it from a Indian or a Chinee or a Potogee. You would buy it from

a black man. And I myself, when I was getting my place in Arouca fix up, I
didn't employ Indian carpenters or masons. If a Indian in Trinidad decide to
go into the carpentering business the man would starve. Who ever see a
Indian carpenter? I suppose the only place in the world where they have
110 Indian carpenters and Indian masons is India. Is a damn funny thing. One of
these days I must make a trip to that country, to just see this thing. And as we
walking I see the names of bakers: Coelho, Pantin, Stauble. Potogee or Swiss,
or something, and then all those other Chinee places. And, look at the
laundries. If a black man open a laundry, you would take your clothes to it? *I*
115 wouldn't take my clothes there. Well, I walking to this restaurant, but I
jumping for joy. And then all sorts of things fit into place. You remember that
the Chinee people didn't let me serve bread across the counter? I uses to
think it was because they didn't trust me with the rush. But it wasn't that. It was
that, if they did let me serve, they would have had no rush at all. You ever see
120 anybody buying their bread off a black man?

I ask Percy why he didn't like black people meddling with his food in public
places. The question throw him a little. He stop and think and say. 'It don't *look*
nice.'

Well, you could guess the rest of the story. Before I went back to Arouca that
125 day I made contact with a yellow boy call Macnab. This boy was half black and
half Chinee, and, though he had a little brown colour and the hair a little curly,
he could pass for one of those Cantonese. They a little darker than the other
Chinee people, I believe. Macnab I find beating a steel pan in somebody yard
– they was practising for Carnival – and I suppose the only reason that Macnab
130 was willing to come all the way to Arouca was because he was short of the
cash to buy his costume for the Carnival island.

But he went up with me. I put him in front of the shop, give him a merino and
a pair of khaki short pants, and tell him to talk as Chinee as he could, if he
wanted to get that Carnival bonus. I stay in the back room, and I start baking
135 bread. I even give Macnab a old Chinee paper, not to read, because Macnab
could scarcely read English, but just to leave lying around, to make it look
good. And I get hold of one of those big Chinese calendars with Chinee
women and flowers and waterfalls and hang it up on the wall. And when this
was all ready, I went down on my knees and thank God. And still the old
140 message coming, but friendly and happy now: 'Youngman, you just bake
bread.'

And, you know, that solve another problem. I was worrying to hell about the
name I should give the place. New Shanghai, Canton, Hongkong, Nanking,
Yang-tse-Kiang. But when the old message came over I know right away what
145 the name should be. I scrub off the old name – no need to tell you what that
was – and I get a proper sign painter to copy a few letters from the Chinee
newspaper. Below that, in big letters, I make him write:

YUNG MAN BAKER

I never show my face in the front of the shop again. And I tell you, without
150 boasting, that I bake damn good bread. And the people of Arouca ain't that
foolish. They know a good thing. And soon I was making so much money that I

was able to open a branch in Arima and then another in Port of Spain self. Was
hard in the beginning to get real Chinee people to work for a black man. But
money have it own way of talking, and when today you pass any of the Yung
155 Man establishments all you seeing behind the counter is Chinee. Some of them
ain't even know they working for a black man. My wife handling that side of
the business, and the wife is Chinee. She come from down Cedros way. So
look at me now, in Port of Spain, giving Stauble and Pantin and Coelho a run
for their money. As I say, I only going in the shops from the back. But every
160 Monday morning I walking brave brave to Marine Square and going in the
bank, from the front.

V S Naipaul

Understanding

What is the nature of the prejudice shown in this story? How is it different from
what is normally thought of as racial prejudice? Do you think this situation
would only happen in the West Indies? Can you think of similar examples in
Britain or other countries?

Would you discriminate against a very young-looking doctor? An elderly
tennis coach? A teacher with a strong accent?

Add possible prejudices to the list.

Writing

1 Write about 300 words on 'The Nature of Prejudice'. Do not confine yourself to
racial prejudice. Include prejudice connected with voice, clothes, manner,
type of job. Consider these prejudices:

> Policemen are nasty. Businessmen work hard. Politicians are liars. Scotsmen
> are mean. Irish people are stupid. Southerners are soft. Yorkshire people
> are blunt. Women are poor drivers. Men can't cook.

Remember that prejudice works two ways. You can be prejudiced in favour as
well as against.

2 Write about an occasion when your views were changed by experience. Most
people will not have such a dramatic experience to recount as Cathy, but a
simple, balanced account of a seemingly unexciting event can be interesting if
it is about a real experience.

Before you begin, read Mark's attempt on the subject (page 98). It appears
exactly as he wrote it, including his mistakes.

2 Write in any way you wish about the experiences suggested by one of the pictures below. You may tell a story, write a conversation or simply describe what you think is happening. Write about 200 words.

Mark's Story

1 'Lets go to Top Man. It's surely the most fashionable clothes shop.'
'Wouldn't it be good to work there? The assistants get paid, and receive free clothes, for standing about with their hands in their pockets.' These were nearly always the first words of conversation my friends and I would say
5 whenever we went on a shopping spree to Cambridge.
Top Man was always the first chouce amongst us as a place to buy clothes. The outward appearance of the shop attracted us to enter and look around. It had 'the look' to make it stand out amongst the other fashion stores, with its gold lettering, chrome stair case, loud 'up-to-date' music and of course the
10 clothes. I always felt a funny tingling as I walked up the stairs to the shop floor.
I think it was, and still is, the shop assistants that used to send us, and no doubt many other people green with envy. Whenever we entered Top Man, or any other fashion store, we were always struck with the impression that all they do is stand about the shop, occasionally approaching a customer or two
15 with, 'Can I help you,' and being paid for doing it in the form of money and clothes. What a great way to earn a living.

Since that time, I've been for a job interview and have now been working in Top Man for nine months. Along with the job I have acquired a different impression in my mind towards the shop, though I thoroughly enjoy working
20 there.
It's true that it is a very popular fashion store; one of the most successful in Europe. We do have a very large and fashionable selection of clothes and can take up to ten thousand pounds in just one week. However, due to my experience of working in the shop as a sales assistant, I now totally disagree
25 with people who say that the assistant is nothing far short of idol. I was shocked to find on my first day of work just how much work there is to do.
The work of the sales assistant is vitally important to the running, maintenance and reputation of the shop. I found, during my first eight or twelve weeks at Top Man, that I had to be put through a series of training
30 programmes. The training totally contradicts the views of many customers, that we ignore them or are unfriendly, for it has taught us that the most important part of the shop is the customer. Through a series of training videos we are taught to be polite, friendly and as helpful as possible to the customer. They also teach us the correct manner in which to approach them; not by
35 saying, 'Can I help?'

Maintenance of the shop is vital to attract the customer and a lot of our time is spent tidying up the clothes, picking up litter, hoovering, thoroughly dusting and cleaning the mirrors. People forget that the shop has a stock room where all the clothes are kept and we are quite often made to spend up to two
40 hours at a time in there sorting out the different types of hangers, a very laborious task. We are continuously running backwards and forwards to the

stock room to find a garment for a customer, even to and from other branches.

During a sale period work becomes doubly hard. We have to go into work on a few Sundays in order to put up posters and advertisments and the tickets
45 on the clothes have to be individually altered to the sale price; a job that can take eight of us all day. The shop is always busier during a sale, making working conditions much more hectic.

Wages are not that high and I don't recieve free clothes. I am paid a normal wage packet for a part-time job and clothes are available to me at twenty-five
50 per cent discount; good, but not free.

Working in a fashion store really isn't as it may appear to a majority of people. People's faces still 'light up' when they hear that you work in Top Man and friends still question me to wheather I get bored standing around or not, even when I come home swelting and totally exhausted.

Comment

Mark has made the subject interesting by recording his feelings in an organised and detailed manner. The account sounds true.

Clumsy expressions

Mark has used some pompous and clumsy expressions. Find simpler alternatives for these.

Top Man was always the first chouce amongst us as a place to buy clothes.
I have acquired a different impression in my mind towards the shop.
The assistant is nothing far short of idol.
Friends still question me to wheather I get bored . . . or not.

Errors

Find Mark's six spelling and three punctuation errors.

⬜▯▷ *LANGUAGE PRACTICE*

Hidden meanings

Each pair of these sentences seems to mean the same, but slight variations in the vocabulary or word order tells us that one sentence in each pair means more than it says.

Find the sentence in each pair that implies criticism and use it in a four-line dialogue to show you have understood its significance.

1 What's the time?
   What time do you call this?

2 What are you doing?
   What do you think you're doing?

3 That's everything I need, I think.
   That's all I needed, I must say.

4 I know you all right. Don't you worry about that.
   I know you. There's no need to be worried.

5 I don't need you to help.
   I don't need any help from you.

6 Are you going to stay here all day, might I ask?
   Can you tell me if you will be here all day?

7 What can you tell me about yourself now?
   Now what have you got to say for yourself?

8 You can talk now.
   It's all right for you to talk.

Stress and meaning

Meaning can be altered simply by stressing different words.

Say these in as many different ways as you can to your neighbour. He or she should reply in a way that shows your meaning has been understood.

   I thought I'd find you here.
   Where did you get that dress?
   I see what he means now.
   I can't understand that.
   I'll teach you to ride my bike.

Play extract

In pairs read this piece from *The Dumb Waiter* by Harold Pinter. Try as many interpretations of the parts as you can. For instance, both men could be joking, or both serious, or one joking and the other serious. Or one could become serious after he realised the other was not joking. You could try variations in volume and tone of voice.

The Dumb Waiter

Ben Go on, go and light it.

Gus Eh?

Ben Go and light it.

Gus Light what?

Ben The kettle.

Gus You mean the gas.

Ben Who does?

Gus You do.

Ben What do you mean, I mean the gas?

Gus Well, that's what you mean, don't you? The gas.

Ben If I say go and light the kettle I mean go and light the kettle.

Gus How can you light a kettle?

Ben It's a figure of speech. Light the kettle. It's a figure of speech.

Gus I've never heard it.

Ben Light the kettle. It's common usage.

Gus I think you've got it wrong.

Ben What do you mean?

Gus They say put on the kettle.

Ben Who says? I have never in all my life heard anyone say put on the kettle.

Gus I bet my mother used to say it.

Ben Your mother? When did you last see your mother?

Gus I don't know, about –

Ben Well, what are you talking about your mother for?

Harold Pinter

The stage directions were removed from this extract. On the next page is the full text. Besides stage instructions, how else has Pinter made the manner and tone of the speaking clear?

Read the extract now as
the dramatist intended.

Ben Go on, go and light it.
Gus Eh?
Ben Go and light it.
Gus Light what?
Ben The kettle.
Gus You mean the gas.
Ben Who does?
Gus You do.
Ben (*his eyes narrowing*). What do you mean, I mean the gas?
Gus Well, that's what you mean, don't you? The gas.
Ben (*powerfully*). If I say go and light the kettle I mean go and light the kettle.
Gus How can you light a kettle?
Ben It's a figure of speech! Light the kettle. It's a figure of speech!
Gus I've never heard it.
Ben Light the kettle! It's common usage!
Gus I think you've got it wrong.
Ben (*menacing*). What do you mean?
Gus They say put on the kettle.
Ben (*taut*). Who says?
　　　They stare at each other, breathing hard.
　　　(*Deliberately.*) I have never in all my life heard anyone say put on the
　　　kettle.
Gus I bet my mother used to say it.
Ben Your mother? When did you last see your mother?
Gus I don't know, about –
Ben Well, what are you talking about your mother for?
　　　They stare.

━━━▭▥▷ *EXAMINATION PRACTICE*

Read this poem and answer the questions below it.

The Man in the Bowler Hat

1   I am the unnoticed, the unnoticeable man:
     The man who sat on your right in the morning train:
     The man you looked through like a window pane:
     The man who was the colour of the carriage, the colour of the mounting
5   Morning pipe-smoke.

     I am the man too busy with a living to live,
     Too hurried and worried to see and smell and touch:
     The man who is patient too long and obeys too much
     And whistles too softly and seldom.

10   I am the man they call the nation's backbone,
     Who am boneless-playable catgut, pliable clay:
     The man they label Little lest one day
     I dare to grow.

     I am the rails on which the moment passes,
15   The megaphone for many words and voices:
     I am graph, diagram,
     Composite face.

     I am the led, the easily fed,
     The tool, the not-quite-fool,
20   The would-be-safe-and-sound
     The uncomplaining, bound,
     The dust fine-ground,
     Stone-for-a-statue waveworn pebble-round.

A J Tessimond

Understanding

1 The poet has used several phrases in the first two verses to emphasise how undistinguished the man in the bowler hat is.

Select three and say why you think the author chose them.

2 In 20–30 words say whether you think the poet approves or disapproves of The Man in the Bowler Hat.

Directed writing

Write in prose a similar piece about *either*

a man or woman who is ambitious, forever looking for opportunities to distinguish himself or herself

or

a man or woman who, unlike the bowler-hatted man, wants to be noticed by everyone, wherever he or she goes.

6 Humour

Gentle and savage

The number of verbs we have to express laughter shows the variety of types of humour: *smiled, chuckled, sneered, mocked, jeered, joked, guffawed, grinned.*

You are asked to

—————→ **Discuss the parts played by situation, character and style in creating humour**

—————→ **Imitate a particular style of humour**

—————→ **Understand satire**

—————→ **Analyse the methods of a satirical passage**

—————→ **Write a satirical passage of your own**

—————→ **Discuss the rights of protest**

—————→ **Extend your range of punctuation**

Examination practice – answer questions on an extract from a play

Adrian Mole falls in love

WEDNESDAY JANUARY 14th

There is a new girl in our class. She sits next to me in Geography. She is all right. Her name is Pandora, but she likes being called 'Box'. Don't ask me why. I might fall in love with her. It's time I fell in love, after all I am $13\frac{3}{4}$ years old.

THURSDAY JANUARY 15th

Pandora has got hair the colour of treacle, and it's long like girls' hair should be. She has quite a good figure. I saw her playing netball and her chest was wobbling. I felt a bit funny. I think this is it!

I am going to bed early to think about Pandora and do my back-stretching exercises. I haven't grown for two weeks. If this carries on I will be a midget.

FRIDAY JANUARY 16th

It was Geography today so I sat next to Pandora for a whole hour. She looks better every day. I told her about her eyes being the same as the dog's. She asked what kind of dog it was. I told her it was a mongrel.

I lent Pandora my blue felt-tip pen to colour round the British Isles.

I think she appreciates these small attentions.

FRIDAY JANUARY 23rd

That is the last time I go to a disco. Everybody there was a punk except me and Rick Lemon, the youth leader. Nigel was showing off all night. He ended up putting a safety pin through his ear. My father had to take him to the hospital in our car.

Pandora has been to see Nigel in hospital. He has got a bit of blood poisoning from the safety pin. Pandora thinks Nigel is dead brave. I think he is dead stupid.

SATURDAY JANUARY 24th

Pandora is going out with Nigel!!!!! I think I will never get over this shock.

SUNDAY JANUARY 25th

THIRD AFTER EPIPHANY

10 a.m. I am ill with all the worry, too weak to write much. Nobody has noticed I haven't eaten any breakfast.

2 p.m. Had two junior aspirins at midday and rallied a bit. Perhaps when I am famous and my diary is discovered people will understand the torment of being a $13\frac{3}{4}$-year-old undiscovered intellectual.

6 p.m. Pandora! My lost love!

Now I will never stroke your treacle hair! (Although my blue felt-tip is still at your disposal.)

8 p.m. Pandora! Pandora! Pandora!

10 p.m. Why? Why? Why?

Midnight. I had a crab-paste sandwich and a satsuma (for the good of my skin). Feel a bit better. I hope Nigel falls off his bike and is squashed flat by a lorry. I will never speak to him again. He knew I was in love with Pandora!

FRIDAY FEBRUARY 13th

It was an unlucky day for me all right!

Pandora doesn't sit next to me in Geography any more. Barry Kent does. He kept copying my work and blowing bubblegum in my ears. I told Miss Elf but she is scared of Barry Kent as well, so she didn't say anything to him.

Pandora looked luscious today, she was wearing a split skirt which showed her legs. She has got a scab on one of her knees. She was wearing Nigel's football scarf round her wrists, but Miss Elf saw it and told her to take it off. Miss Elf is not scared of Pandora. I have sent her a Valentine's Day card (Pandora, not Miss Elf).

SATURDAY FEBRUARY 14th

I only got one Valentine's Day card. It was in my mother's handwriting so it doesn't count. My mother had a massive card delivered, it was so big that a GPO van had to bring it to the door. She went all red when she opened the envelope and saw the card. It was dead good. There was a big satin elephant holding a bunch of plastic flowers in its trunk and a bubble coming out of its mouth saying 'Hi, Honey Bun! I ain't never gonna forget you!' There was no name written inside, just drawings of hearts with 'Pauline' written inside them. My father's card was very small and had a bunch of purple flowers on the front. My father had written on the inside 'Let's try again'.

Here is the poem I wrote inside Pandora's card.

Pandora!

I adore ya.

I implore ye

Don't ignore me.

I wrote it left-handed so that she wouldn't know it was from me.

WEDNESDAY JUNE 10th

Pandora and I are in love! It is official!! She told Claire Neilson, who told me.

I told Nigel to tell Claire to tell Pandora that I return her love. I am over the moon with joy and rapture. I can overlook the fact that Pandora smokes five Benson and Hedges a day and has her own lighter. When you are in love such things cease to matter.

The Secret Diary of Adrian Mole Aged 13¾ by Sue Townsend

Discussion in small groups

1 What makes these particular quotations funny?

> It's time I fell in love, after all I am 13¾ years old.
> I haven't grown for two weeks. If this carries on I will be a midget.
> I think she appreciates these small attentions.
> Pandora thinks Nigel is dead brave. I think he is dead stupid.
> Had two junior aspirins at midday . . .
> 8 p.m. Pandora! Pandora! Pandora!
> 10 p.m. Why? Why? Why?
> Midnight. I had a crab-paste sandwich and a satsuma.
> She has got a scab on one of her knees.
> It was in my mother's handwriting so it doesn't count.
> Pandora and I are in love! It is official!! She told Clare Neilson, who told me.
> I can overlook the fact that Pandora smokes five Benson and Hedges a day
> and has her own lighter.

2 Which other quotations amuse you? Why?

3 What kind of boy is Adrian Mole? Does his character contribute to the humour?

4 Which age groups would *The Secret Diary of Adrian Mole* appeal to most, and which least?

5 What is the *tone* of the diary? Does it vary? How does the tone contribute to the humour?

Drawing conclusions

Using what you have found so far, decide on your three chief reasons why you find Adrian Mole's diary funny. Compare your reasons with those of other groups.

Writing

1 Imagine that Adrian has written a letter to a problem page, explaining that Pandora is going out with Nigel and asking for advice. Write the letter, imitating his *style* and *tone* as closely as you can.

2 We are given a little insight into Miss Elf's life: she is as scared of Barry Kent as Adrian is.

Sue Townsend has written a comic book by exaggerating the typical problems of adolescence. Attempt your own comic piece by exaggerating the typical problems of a teacher. Write a week's entries in his/her diary.

A Modest Proposal for Preventing the Children of Ireland from Being a Burden to Their Country

The following piece is unpleasant to read; it was meant to be.
   Three hundred years ago in Ireland thousands of people were dying of cold and famine; yet a few were wealthy.

The author, Jonathan Swift, felt that his countrymen were being cruelly exploited by politicians, both in Ireland and England. He wanted to shock them into seeing their responsibilities.
   Remember, as you read the piece, that Swift is not serious about the content, but very serious about his purpose.

Imagine you were a politician responsible for governing Ireland at the time. How would you react to the piece?

1   It is an unpleasant sight to people travelling in this country to see crowds of
   female beggars, followed by three, four or six children clad in rags, all
   troubling every passer-by for food.
      I think everyone would agree that the huge number of children is a great
5   additional burden for this country to bear. Therefore whoever could find a
   cheap, fair and easy way of making these children useful members of the
   country would deserve to have his statue set up as a preserver of the nation.
      I have thought for many years on this important problem and now have a
   solution to offer. A child just dropped from its dam can live on her milk for
10 almost a year, supplemented by the shilling or two the mother may receive
   from begging. It is exactly at one year old that my scheme will provide for the
   children, so that instead of being a burden to their parents, or wanting food
   and clothing from the Government, they will contribute to the feeding and
   partly to the clothing of thousands of people.
15   Another great advantage of my scheme is that it will prevent women ridding
   themselves of their unwanted children by abortion or, even worse, murder,
   sacrificing their poor innocent babes to avoid the expense of their upkeep,
   something which moves tears and pity in the most savage of human beings.

      There are one-and-a-half million people in this country, about two hundred
20 thousand couples where the wife is a breeder. About thirty thousand of these
   are able to feed their children, so that leaves a hundred and seventy thousand
   breeders. Take away about fifty thousand who miscarry or whose children die
   of neglect or disease. There remains about one hundred and twenty thousand
   children born of poor parents in every year.
25   How can this number be reared and provided for? I shall now humbly

propose my idea, which I hope will not be liable to the least objection.

I have been assured by a very knowing American acquaintance, that a young healthy child at a year old is a most delicious, nourishing and wholesome food, whether stewed, roasted, baked or boiled; I'm sure that it 30 will serve equally well in a Fricassée or a Ragoût.
I therefore humbly offer it to public consideration that of the hundred and twenty thousand children available each year, twenty thousand should be reserved for breeding, only a fourth males, which is more than we allow to sheep, cattle or swine. The remaining hundred thousand may be offered for 35 sale to people of quality and wealth, providing the mother feeds them plentifully in the last month so as to render them plump for a good table. A child will make two dishes at a party for friends and, when the family dines alone the fore and hind quarters will make a reasonable dish, and the carcass seasoned with a little pepper and salt will be very good boiled later for a stew 40 or soup.

I admit that this food will be expensive and therefore most likely to be bought by landlords. They have already devoured most of the parents so they seem to have the best right to the children.
The cost of nursing a beggar's child is about two shillings a year (in the list 45 of beggars I include common labourers and four fifths of the farmers) and I believe there will be many gentlemen who would give ten shillings for the carcass of a good fat child, which, as I have said, will make four nutritious meals. So the mother will have eight shillings clear profit and will no longer be a burden on the country. She will also be fit and strong enough for work 50 between the bearing of her children.
If it be argued that infant flesh would be dear in comparison to beef and mutton I would point out that the skin of a child's carcass will make admirable gloves for ladies and boots for fine gentlemen.
Slaughterhouses could be set up in the most convenient places in our major 55 cities and I have been assured that there are plenty of butchers seeking work; although I would personally recommend buying children alive, and dressing them hot from the knife, as we do roasting pigs.

I can think of no objection that can possibly be raised against this proposal, unless it is that the numbers of people in the country will be lessened. But this 60 is an objection that only politicians would make. Any politician who dislikes my scheme should ask the parents of these children whether they would not consider it a great happiness to have been sold for food themselves when they were young, and so avoided a life of misery through the oppression of landlords, the impossibility of paying rent, the lack of basic food, clothes for 65 their backs and a hovel to shelter.
Finally I wish to stress that I have only the public good at heart in proposing my scheme. I have no personal interest, since I have no children from which I could make a profit, the youngest being nine and my wife past child-bearing.

Jonathan Swift

The writer's aim

The writer's intention is to shame the politicians and the wealthy for their
neglect of the poor.

He tries to achieve his intention by saying the very opposite. This is called
irony. We all use simple irony, saying *How clever!* to someone who has spilt a
drink or *Brilliant!* to an unfortunate goalkeeper who has let the ball through his
legs. Swift's use of irony is more subtle and savage. He proposes that the rich
should exploit the poor even further, using them like farm animals. By
suggesting monstrous cruelty, he is trying to shock the politicians and the rich
into seeing their present cruelties and neglect.

The passage is a savage and bitter attack on the government of the time.

Understanding the passage

1 How does the writer suggest in the third paragraph that his scheme should be
   taken very seriously? How does he give a hint that his scheme will involve
   treating poor people like animals?
2 In paragraph 5 the author gives several sets of figures. What does he wish to
   show about himself and his scheme by this paragraph?
3 How does the writer pretend in paragraph 6 that he is quite unconscious of the
   monstrous cruelty of his scheme?
4 At last the scheme is revealed. Why did he spend so long recommending it
   and making it sound reasonable?
5 How does paragraph 8 make it clear that the poor are to be used like animals?
   What horrible details does the writer introduce in a casual way? What is the
   effect of this casual manner?
6 Why, according to the author, would most poor people in Ireland wish the
   scheme in operation when they were children?
   What is the real purpose of the author in ignoring the reasons for the blessing
   of an early death?

Language

For each group of phrases, pick out the one the author has used and say why he used it in preference to the others.

a) *begging* every passer-by/*troubling* every passer-by/*asking* every passer-by
b) the wife is a breeder/the wife is able to bear children
c) to render them *flabby*/to render them *fat*/to render them *plump*
d) the *carcass*/the *body*/the *trunk* of a child
e) *devoured* most of the parents/*eaten* most of the parents
f) recently killed/hot from the knife/only just dead
g) I wish to *say*/I wish to *explain*/I wish to *stress*

Satire – write your own piece

This type of writing is called satire. Its aim is to make anything from an idea to a system of government seem absurd. What is not changed by argument might be changed by ridicule – nobody likes to be laughed at, particularly in the savage and bitter manner of *A Modest Proposal*.

Before you attempt a piece of satire yourself, read this by a person of your own age.

Parents

My parents have always been a great help to me. They know I have poor eyesight so they are always pointing out things to me. They tell me that the washing-up is waiting to be done, my bedroom floor is covered with clothes and books, and that the lawn needs cutting. I would never have noticed these things if I hadn't such kind parents.

One thing they have really taught me well is to tell the time. My mum shouts, 'It's eight o'clock' to me every morning. Sometimes I get little tests as an extra help. They ask me, 'What time do you call this?' when I come home at night.

My dad is very anxious that I shouldn't get burned, so he shields the fire from me by sitting on top of it when he comes in. He also kindly makes sure I understand what he says because he nearly always shouts when he speaks to me.

I can't think of the words to describe what my life would be without my parents' help. Perhaps 'very happy' might do.

Try a piece of satire on one of these subjects.

Parents   Football fans   Factory farming   Teachers   Work   The police

Discussion

Making a protest

A Modest Proposal is a bitter protest against the authorities Swift thinks are responsible for the plight of Ireland's poor. The basis of the protest is savage laughter.

Today there are many forms of protest, some more physical than letters or pamphlets such as *A Modest Proposal.* In the 1980s people lie down in roads, camp outside nuclear establishments, go on strike, starve themselves or even burn themselves to death – all for their particular cause.

What is the most effective form of protest? Are there any types of protest that should be banned? Are there any causes so bad that you think protesting on their behalf should not be allowed? What should the authorities' reaction be to protests?

Writing – respond to a protest

Choose a recent protest reported in the local or national press. Write to the newspaper giving your reasons for supporting or opposing the protest.

Writing – odd situations

Write 150–200 words on one of the pictures on the opposite page.
What is happening? Write either as an observer or one of the people involved.

▭▬▷ *LANGUAGE PRACTICE*

Extend your punctuation

Most writers use only two punctuation marks. If you wish to extend your range, study the uses of these four.

Colon

1 A way of introducing direct speech:
   I called to the gaoler: 'Let him out at once.'

2 For expanding on a previous statement:
   Pockets of resistance sprang up all over the country: there were soon thirty towns and cities in revolt.

3 As a substitute for *namely*:
   George Brown had many fine qualities: wit, compassion, determination and courage.

Semi-colon

1 When you need a slightly longer pause than a comma, but where a full stop would make too strong a break.

   For example:
   Every morning the work of washing the floor, dousing the walls and polishing the brasses took over two hours; I just did not have the strength to keep it up.

   The semi-colon gives the reader time to pause over the tasks and emphasises that the writer could not accomplish them properly.

2 Where you want to balance or contrast two parts of a sentence:
   I would have made a scene if my car was damaged; that he said nothing aroused my suspicions.

3 In a list of closely connected items:
   He felt for his pen; he discovered it had gone; John began to run; the policeman set off in pursuit.

   In this example commas could not be used instead of the semi-colons, but the writer does not want the strong pauses that full stops would give.

Dash

1 Used in pairs to separate a subordinate part of a sentence – a substitute for brackets:
   How dare you – a person of your reputation – commit such a stupid crime!

2 To give emphasis at the end of a sentence, especially a climax or something unexpected:

> Joe hit the ball past the fielder, ran the first one quickly, turned and checked his stride – a fatal hesitation.

3 Used in dialogue to show a breaking-off or hesitation:

   a) 'I will meet you at – '
   'Don't trouble yourself.'

   b) 'I – don't – think – I – dare.'

Brackets

Used to mark off a subordinate part of a sentence.
Study these three examples:

1 The horses, which had worked for three hours, were at last rested.

2 The man over there – I don't think you know him – was a pilot during the war.

3 Jane always woke her father with a shake at six (her mother had died when she was a child) as he was a sound sleeper and was liable to snore through the alarm.

Pairs of commas, dashes and brackets are used to divide off the subordinate parts of the sentences.
Notice that commas provide the weakest divide and brackets the most complete. Your choice will be decided by how complete an 'aside' the subordinate part is.

Punctuation practice

Punctuate these sentences in what you consider the most appropriate way.

1 The door would not open the catch was jammed.

2 Jane tested the plank it seemed wobbly she dare not take the risk the water looked icy cold.

3 My father I hope he is wrong says I have no chance of passing.

4 You will need all your equipment strong shoes a stout rope waterproof clothing and a small ridge tent.

5 The following day Alison I'd not seen her for five years was pictured on the front page of the local paper.

6 Sometimes he looks neat and tidy usually he is a scruffy mess.

Professional writers and punctuation

Famous writers use a full range of punctuation marks. Here are the openings of five famous novels with the punctuation removed. Below each are listed the punctuation marks that were used. Copy them out putting in the marks where you think they should be. Compare your punctuation with the original, by taking the book from the library.

   Before using semi-colons, colons, dashes or brackets, check the lists above to find the type of usage which best fits the circumstance.

Moll Flanders

My true name is so well known in the records or registers at Newgate and in the Old Bailey and there are some things of such consequence still depending there relating to my particular conduct that it is not to be expected I should set my name or the account of my family to this work perhaps after my death it may be better known at present it would not be proper no not though a general pardon should be issued even without exceptions of persons or crimes.

Daniel Defoe

7 commas 2 semi-colons

The Time Machine

The Time Traveller for so it will be convenient to speak of him was expounding a recondite matter to us his grey eyes shone and twinkled and his usually pale face was flushed and animated the fire burned brightly and the soft radiance of the incandescent lights in the lilies of silver caught in the bubbles that flashed and passed in our glasses our chairs being his patents embraced and caressed us rather than submitted to be sat upon and there was that luxurious after-dinner atmosphere when thought runs gracefully free of the trammels of precision and he put it to us in this way marking the points with a lean forefinger as we sat and lazily admired his earnestness over this new paradox as we thought it and his fecundity.

H G Wells

5 full stops 5 commas 2 pairs of brackets 1 pair of dashes

Emma

Emma Woodhouse handsome clever and rich with a comfortable home and happy disposition seemed to unite some of the best blessings of existence and had lived nearly twenty-one years in the world with very little to distress or vex her.

Jane Austen

5 commas 1 semi-colon

Goodbye to All That

Nor had I any illusions about Algernon Charles Swinburne who often used to stop my perambulator when he met it on Nurses' Walk at the edge of Wimbledon Common and pat me on the head and kiss me he was an inveterate pram-stopper and patter and kisser Nurses' Walk lay between 'The Pines' Putney where he lived with Watts-Dunton and the Rose and Crown public house where he went for his daily pint of beer Watts-Dunton allowed him twopence for it and no more.

Robert Graves

1 full stop 6 commas 1 colon 1 semi-colon 1 pair of brackets

Jane Eyre

There was no possibility of taking a walk that day we had been wandering indeed in the leafless shrubbery an hour in the morning but since dinner Mrs Reed when there was no company dined early the cold winter wind had brought with it clouds so sombre and a rain so penetrating that further outdoor exercise was now out of the question
   I was glad of it I never liked long walks especially on chilly afternoons dreadful to me was the coming home in the raw twilight with nipped fingers and toes and a heart saddened by the chidings of Bessie the nurse and humbled by the consciousness of my physical inferiority to Eliza, John and Georgiana Reed.

Charlotte Brontë

2 full stops 12 commas 1 semi-colon 2 colons 1 pair of brackets

▭▭▭▷ *EXAMINATION PRACTICE*

Read this extract from *The Royal Pardon* by John Arden. A company of travelling actors are rehearsing their version of King Arthur. They start with the scene in which Sir Lancelot confesses that he is in love with King Arthur's Queen, Guinevere.

The company consists of Mr Croke, the manager; his wife; two young actors, William and Esmeralda; and Charles, who usually plays the clown's part.

The Royal Pardon

Croke (*jumping up decisively*) Yes, well, now then, to work! Scripts,   1
Esmeralda darling, scripts, properties, we need the rose-trellis,
where is it? Set it up, my dear, no delays now – we rehearse!
(*Esmeralda hands out scripts and brings in the trellis, which is
rather shaky and she finds it difficult to erect it.*)   5
Guinevere, sitting down. Lancelot beside her, thus, the palm of
his hand upon the back of her hand, thus – I think that's how we
used to play it. We'll start from 'a double passion'. Don't bother
with the trellis, child, it's only making difficulties, we'll carry on
without. Ha ha, let me see –   10
    A double passion wars within my breast.
    Now that my love for thee has been confessed
    My duty to King Arthur must needs fly.
    He is my Lord, for whom I once would die.
    Alas, he is thy husband too. 'Tis plain   15
    If I am not his enemy, he is mine.
Mrs Croke   Nay, should he find us here his angry blade
    Must pierce thy heart and thou on turf be laid.
    Sweet knight, there is such peril in thy devotion.
    I sorely fear it will destroy this nation.   20
Croke   Yet am I not still loyal to the crown?
    I swear it, by this rose that I pluck down!
No, no, it's altogether too difficult to do it without props. I must
have the rose – I have to smell it and kiss it, and put it in your
bosom and so forth – trellis, Esmeralda, trellis, if you please.   25
The imagery of the rose is of prime importance to this scene –
William, are you watching? You may find yourself playing
Lancelot one of these days; learn, me boy, learn – there's a
tradition in this part, you know, as in all the great classic parts –
we ignore it at our peril.   30
(*Esmeralda has set up the trellis.*)
Good, good, try again –

I swear it, by this rose that I pluck down – !
(*In endeavouring to pluck the rose from the trellis, he finds it
is too firmly fastened on. The whole trellis sways dangerously.*) 35
Oh, for heaven's sake – when was this last used? Who's been
looking after the props? Esmeralda, really, this is frankly quite
ridiculous! I cannot possibly continue with this scene until the
whole thing's been overhauled. Not just now, dear, not just
now – we'll carry on from somewhere else. We'll get on to the 40
discovery. Mordred, the villain, brings in King Arthur to
observe the guilty couple. William, are you ready? I'll give you
your cue:
　　But hark, I hear a footstep on the sward.
　　No matter, I have my weapon, I am on guard. 45
William, I am on guard. But against whom, might I ask?

William	It's not quite King Arthur yet. Mordred comes on first.
Croke	Well, where is he? Where is Mordred?
Esmeralda	You haven't cast him yet, Mr Croke.
Croke	Oh, Charles. Leave those sandwiches alone for a moment, and 50 pick up a script.
Charles	What, me, to play the villain?
Mrs Croke	Impossible. Do have some sense, Antonius. This isn't a comic villain, you know. I don't see how Charles can conceivably –
Croke	Then who do you suggest, my love? We are but a small 55 company.
Esmeralda	I'll have a go. I've played breeches parts before. And he is meant to be a young man. Is that all right? Shall I enter? Mr Croke?
Croke	Can you fight? There is a battle in the last act. Otherwise I 60 don't –
Mrs Croke	Let her try it, at any rate. You'd better take your skirt off. (*Esmeralda takes off her skirt – she has tights on under it.*) She'll have to double with the lady-in-waiting in Act Two – I must have the lady-in-waiting or my entire 65 hysterical scene will go for nothing. Remember I have to slap her, it's my best moment in the whole play. So carry on, my dear, roll your eyes and don't forget to swagger. You'll be wearing a sword-belt, of course.
Croke	Just one moment. If Esmeralda is going to play the villain, 70 and really, you know, there is no reason why she shouldn't because apart from the battle it's not a very large part – who is going to be Merlin?
Mrs Croke	Can we not cut Merlin, my love?
Croke	I don't think so – he's most important – he has to warn Lancelot 75 about the – no no, we can't cut him. It would be better to cut the lady-in-waiting if we have to . . . I have it. I can double Merlin with Lancelot, play it myself. A white beard, sky-blue mantle, throw it over my armour – the

character is attractive – sophisticated, whimsical, rather   80
terrifying when he prophesies. I've never played him.
It's a challenge.

Esmeralda They have a conversation.

Croke Who has a conversation?

Esmeralda Merlin and Lancelot. They have a conversation.   85

John Arden

Understanding

1 What do the stage directions about the rose trellis show us of Mr Croke's character? Quote from the passage to support your answer.

2 What contrast is there between Mr Croke's opinion of his acting abilities and the evidence in the passage? Quote to support your answer.

3 What advice about tone of voice and manner would you give the actor playing Esmeralda when she delivers these lines?

'You haven't cast him yet, Mr Croke.' (line 49)
'They have a conversation.' (line 83)

Give reasons for your advice.

4 'Anti-climax is the main source of humour in the passage.'
By reference to the passage say whether you agree or disagree with this statement.

5 'A selfish snob.'
Do you agree with this comment on Mrs Croke? Give reasons.

6 Basing your answer on Mr Croke's character as shown in the extract, write his reply to the problem Esmeralda points out at the end of the passage.

7 Use your imagination

Murder most foul

There are many situations that a writer will never experience for him- or herself. He or she must imagine how people would react in such situations.

You are asked to

→ **Study and interpret a section of a play after a murder**

→ **Read the lines in pairs to explore the way tension is created**

→ **Write an imaginary diary extract for the murderers**

→ **Understand a prose account of a murder**

→ **Compare the substance and style of the play and prose accounts**

→ **Consider the effect of imagery**

→ **Study a modern murder story**

→ **Study two versions of a ballad**

→ **Discuss the need for a 'happy ending'**

→ **Extend your vocabulary**

Examination practice – answer questions on a poem

Killing the King

In order to become King himself, Macbeth has just killed Duncan, King of Scotland, at night while he was asleep. He should also have smeared Duncan's guards with the blood so that the blame would fall on them. Lady Macbeth has previously drugged the guards.

Macbeth (*Within*) Who's there? – what, ho!		1
Lady M Alack, I am afraid they have awaked,		
And 't is not done: – the attempt, and not the deed,		
Confounds us. – Hark! – I laid their daggers ready;		
He could not miss them. – Had he not resembled		5
My father as he slept, I had done't. – My husband!		
(*Enter Macbeth carrying bloodstained daggers*)		
Macbeth I have done the deed. – Didst thou not hear a noise?		
Lady M I heard the owl scream, and the crickets cry.		
Did not you speak?		
Macbeth When?		
Lady M Now.		
Macbeth As I descended?		10
Lady M Ay.		
Macbeth Hark!		
Who lies i' the second chamber?		
Lady M Donalbain.		
Macbeth (*Looks on his hands*) This is a sorry sight.		
Lady M A foolish thought, to say a sorry sight.		
Macbeth There's one did laugh in 's sleep, and one cried 'Murder!'		15
That they did wake each other: I stood and heard them;		
But they did say their prayers, and addressed them		
Again to sleep.		
Lady M There are two lodged together.		
Macbeth One cried 'God bless us!' and, 'Amen!' the other,		
As they had seen me with these hangman's hands.		20
Listening their fear, I could not say 'Amen',		
When they did say 'God bless us!'		
Lady M Consider it not so deeply.		
Macbeth But wherefore could not I pronounce 'Amen'?		
I had most need of blessing, and 'Amen'		
Stuck in my throat.		
Lady M These deeds must not be thought		25
After these ways: so, it will make us mad.		
Macbeth Methought I heard a voice cry, 'Sleep no more!		

Macbeth does murder sleep', – the innocent sleep;
Sleep, that knits up the ravelled sleave of care,
The death of each day's life, sore labour's bath,   30
Balm of hurt minds, great nature's second course,
Chief nourisher in life's feast; –

Lady M   What do you mean?
Macbeth Still it cried 'Sleep no more!' to all the house:
'Glamis hath murdered sleep, and therefore Cawdor
Shall sleep no more, Macbeth shall sleep no more.'   35
Lady M Who was it that thus cried? Why, worthy thane,

You do unbend your noble strength, to think
So brainsickly of things. Go, get some water,
And wash this filthy witness from your hand.
Why did you bring these daggers from the place?   40
They must lie there; go, carry them, and smear
The sleepy grooms with blood.

Macbeth   I'll go no more:
I am afraid to think what I have done;
Look on 't again I dare not.

Lady M   Infirm of purpose!
Give me the daggers. The sleeping and the dead   45
Are but as pictures; 't is the eye of childhood
That fears a painted devil. If he do bleed,
I'll gild the faces of the grooms withal,
For it must seem their guilt. (*Exit. Knock within*)

Macbeth   Whence is that knocking?
How is 't with me, when every noise appals me?   50
What hands are here? Ha! They pluck out mine eyes.
Will all great Neptune's ocean wash this blood
Clean from my hand? No, this my hand will rather
The multitudinous seas incarnadine,
Making the green one red.   55

(*Re-enter Lady Macbeth*)

Lady M My hands are of your colour; but I shame
To wear a heart so white. (*Knock within*) I hear a knocking
At the south entry: retire we to our chamber.
A little water clears us of this deed:
How easy is it then!   60

William Shakespeare

Understanding the characters

Macbeth

Answer these questions as if you were Macbeth.

1 Why do you look at your hands and call them 'a sorry sight'?
2 What did you hear from the second chamber?
3 Why do you call your hands 'these hangman's hands'?
4 Why do you think you cannot say 'Amen'?
5 What is the importance of sleep to you?
6 You do not literally mean that you have murdered sleep. What do you mean?
7 Why will you not go back to smear Duncan's grooms with blood?
8 Again, you do not literally mean that even the ocean cannot clean the blood from your hands. What do you mean?

9 What is your final reaction to the murder of Duncan?

Lady Macbeth

Answer these questions as if you were Lady Macbeth.

1 When you hear Macbeth calling, what do you fear?
2 Why didn't you kill Duncan when you were laying out the grooms' daggers?
3 What makes you exclaim 'My husband!'?
4 What do you try to do when Macbeth looks at his hands and says, 'This is a sorry sight'?
5 Why do you tell your husband, 'Consider it not so deeply'?
6 What warning do you give your husband if he continues to dwell on the murder?
7 How do you respond when Macbeth says he will not go back to the grooms?
8 What do you accuse Macbeth of?
9 How do you try to calm down your husband when he is hysterically convinced that he will never be rid of the blood?
10 What action do you take to cover up the murders?

Discussion – the relationship between the Macbeths

Which of the two would you expect to have planned the murder? Why?
Lady Macbeth warns *it will make us mad.* Which of the two would you expect to go mad first? Why?
Which do you think is the stronger of the pair?
Do you think they will enjoy being King and Queen?
The contrast between their two characters is important for creating interest in the drama. What are the contrasts between them?

Creating suspense

In pairs practise the first ten lines of the extract. Make your cues fast. That is, speak your line almost before the other person has finished. Do you find any difference in effect between the first seven lines spoken by Lady Macbeth and the remaining three which are broken up between the two speakers? What is the effect in these last lines?

Writing a diary

Imagine that the Macbeths each confide their secrets to their diaries. Write either Lady Macbeth's or Macbeth's account of the murder, using as much detail from the extract as you can.

The flight of Sikes

Bill Sikes, a burglar, has killed his girlfriend Nancy because he thinks she has betrayed him. Now he must get rid of the evidence.

1 Of all bad deeds that, under cover of the darkness, had been committed within wide London's bounds since night hung over it, that was the worst. Of all the horrors that rose with an ill scent upon the morning air, that was the foulest and most cruel.

5   The sun – the bright sun, that brings back, not light alone, but new life, and hope, and freshness to man – burst upon the crowded city in clear and radiant glory. Through costly-coloured glass and paper-mended window, through cathedral dome and rotten crevice, it shed its equal ray. It lighted up the room where the murdered woman lay. It did. He tried to shut it out, but it would

10 stream in. If the sight had been a ghastly one in the dull morning, what was it, now, in all that brilliant light!

   He had not moved; he had been afraid to stir. There had been a moan and motion of the hand; and, with terror added to rage, he had struck and struck again. Once he threw a rug over it; but it was worse to fancy the eyes, and

15 imagine them moving towards him, than to see them glaring upward, as if

watching the reflection of the pool of gore that quivered and danced in the sunlight on the ceiling. He had plucked it off again. And there was the body – mere flesh and blood, no more – but such flesh, and so much blood!

He struck a light, kindled a fire, and thrust the club into it.

20   There was hair upon the end, which blazed and shrunk into a light cinder, and, caught by the air, whirled up the chimney. Even that frightened him, sturdy as he was; but he held the weapon till it broke, and then piled it on the coals to burn away, and smoulder into ashes. He washed himself, and rubbed his clothes; there were spots that would not be removed, but he cut the pieces
25 out, and burnt them. How those stains were dispersed about the room! The very feet of the dog were bloody.

    All this time he had never once turned his back upon the corpse; no, not for a moment. Such preparations completed, he moved, backward, towards the door: dragging the dog with him, lest he should soil his feet anew and carry
30 out new evidence of the crime into the streets. He shut the door softly, locked it, took the key, and left the house.

    He crossed over, and glanced up at the window, to be sure that nothing was visible from the outside. There was the curtain still drawn, which she would have opened to admit the light she never saw again. It lay nearly under there.
35 *He* knew that. God, how the sun poured down upon the very spot!

    The glance was instantaneous. It was a relief to have got free of the room. He whistled on the dog, and walked rapidly away.

Oliver Twist by Charles Dickens

Understanding the passage

1 How does Dickens manage to make the first paragraph sound like an accusation?
2 What does the sun represent? Why does Sikes want to shut it out?
3 What is Sikes' first reaction to the murder?
4 Why does he keep striking at the body?
5 Why does Dickens choose to have Sikes frightened by Nancy's eyes in particular?
6 What steps does Sikes take to conceal the murder?
7 How does Dickens suggest Sikes' terror about the murder when he is on the run?

Play and novel compared

Neither Shakespeare nor Dickens was a murderer. Yet they both had the power to imagine and create a murderer's mind. Using both passages make notes about what a murderer feels after the deed. From your notes write a short piece about the feelings of a murderer.

Imagery

Both writers have the power to create memorable images. What images stay in your mind? Explain why they are effective in suggesting a murderer's feelings. (See page 137 for an explanation of imagery.)

The differences

1 What is the most obvious difference between the two extracts?
2 How do we learn what Sikes is thinking and feeling?
3 How do we know what the Macbeths are thinking and feeling?

JUSTIFIABLE HOMICIDE?

This is a legal term. What do you think it means?

Read this modern story and decide what your verdict would be if the boy
were caught and brought to trial.

Drunkard of the River

1   'Where you' father?'
     The boy did not answer. He paddled his boat carefully between the
shallows, and then he ran the boat alongside the bank, putting his paddle in
front to stop it. Then he threw the rope round the picket and helped himself on
5 to the bank. His mother stood in front the door still staring at him.
     'Where you' father?'
     The boy disguised his irritation. He looked at his mother and said calmly,
'You know Pa. You know where he is.'
     'And ah did tell you not to come back without 'im?'
10   'I could bring Pa back?' The boy cried. His bitterness was getting the better
of him. 'When Pa want to drink I could bring him back?'

It was always the same. The boy's mother stood in front of the door staring up the river. Every Saturday night it was like this. Every Saturday night Mano went out to the village and drank himself helpless and lay on the floor of the
15 shop, cursing and vomiting until the Chinaman was ready to close up. Then they rolled him outside and heaven knows, maybe they even spat on him.

The boy's mother stared up the river, her face twisted with anger and distress. She couldn't go up the river now. It would be hell and fire if she went. But Mano had to be brought home. She turned to see what the boy was doing.
20 He had packed away the things from the shopping bag and he was now reclining on the settee.

'You have to go for you' father, you know,' she said.

'Who?'

'You!'

25 'Not me!'

'Who de hell you tellin' not me,' she shouted. She was furious now. 'Dammit, you have to go for you' father!'

Sona had risen from the settee on the alert. His mother hardly ever hit him now but he could never tell. It had been a long time since she had looked so
30 angry and had stamped her feet.

He rose slowly and reluctantly and as he glanced at her he couldn't understand what was wrong with her. He couldn't see why she bothered about his father at all. For his father was stupid and worthless and made their life miserable. If he could have had his way Mano would have been out of the
35 house a long time now. His bed would have been the dirty meat-table in front of Assing's shop. That was what he deserved. The rascal! The boy spat through the window. The very thought of his father sickened him.

Yet with Sona's mother it was different. The man she had married and who had turned out badly was still the pillar of her life. Although he had piled up
40 grief after grief, tear after tear, she felt lost and drifting without him. To her he was as mighty as the very Ortoire that flowed outside. She remembered that in his young days there was nothing any living man could do that he could not.

In her eyes he was still young. He did not grow old. It was she who had aged. He had only turned out badly. She hated him for the way he drank rum
45 and squandered the little money he worked for. But she did not mind the money so much. It was seeing him drunk. She knew when he arrived back staggering how she would shake with rage and curse him, but even so, how inside she would shake with the joy of having him safe and home.

She wondered what was going on at the shop now. She wondered if he was
50 already drunk and helpless and making a fool of himself.

With Sona, the drunkard's son, this was what stung more than ever. The way Mano, his father, cursed everybody and made a fool of himself. Sometimes he had listened to his father and he had felt to kick him, so ashamed he was. Often in silence he had shaken his fist and said, 'One day, ah'll – ah'll . . .'
55 He had watched his mother put up with hell and sweat and starvation. She

132

was getting skinnier every day, and she looked more like fifty-six than the thirty-six she was. Already her hair was greying. Sometimes he had looked at her and, thinking of his father, he had ground his teeth and had said, 'Beast!' several times to himself. He was in that frame of mind now. Bitter and reluctant,
60 he went to untie the boat.

'If I can't bring 'im, I'll leave 'im,' he said angrily.

'Get somebody to help you!'

He turned to her. 'Nobody wouldn't help me. He does insult everybody. Last week Bolai kick him.'

65 'Bolai kick 'im? An' what you do?'

His mother was stung with rage and shock. Her eyes were large and red and watery.

The boy casually unwound the rope from the picket. 'What I do?' he said. 'That is he and Bolai business.'

70 His mother burst out crying.

'What ah must do?' the boy said. 'All the time ah say, "Pa, come home, come home, Pa!" You know what he tell me? He say, "Go to hell, yuh little bitch!"'

His mother turned to him. Beads of tears were still streaming down the sides of her face.

75 'Sona, go for you' father. Go now. You stand up dey and watch Bolai kick you' father and you ent do nothing? He mind you, you know,' she sobbed. 'He is you' father, you ungrateful – – –' And choking with anger and grief she burst out crying again.

When she raised her head, Sona was paddling towards mid-stream,
80 scowling, avoiding the shallows of the river.

True enough there was havoc in Assing's shop. Mano's routine was well under way. He staggered about the bar dribbling and cursing and yet again the Chinaman spoke to him about his words, not that he cared about Mano's behaviour. The rum Mano consumed made quite a difference to Assing's
85 account. It safe-guarded Mano's free speech in the shop.

But the customers were disgusted. All sorts of things had happened on Saturday nights through Mano's drunkenness. There was no such thing as buying in peace once Mano was there.

So now with trouble looming, the coming of Sona was sweet relief. As Sona
90 walked in, someone pointed out his father between the sugar bags.

'Pa!'

Mano looked up. 'What you come for?' he drawled. 'Who send you?'

'Ma say to come home,' Sona said. He told himself that he mustn't lose control in front of strangers.
95 'Well!'

'Ma send me for you.'

'You! You' mother send you for me! So you is me father now, eh – eh?' In his drunken rage the old man staggered towards his son.

Sona didn't walk back. He never did anything that would make him feel
100 stupid in front of a crowd. But before he realised what was happening his father lunged forward and struck him on his left temple.

'So you is me father, eh? You is me father, now!' He kicked the boy.

Two or three people bore down on Mano and held him off the boy. Sona put
105 his hands to his belly where his father had just kicked him. Tears came to his eyes. The drunkenness was gripping Mano more and more. He could hardly stand on his own now. He was struggling to set himself free. The men held on to him. Sona kept out of the way.

'It's a damn' shame!' somebody said.

'Shame?' Mano drawled. 'An' he is me father now, 'e modder send him for
110 me. Let me go,' he cried, struggling more than ever, 'I'll kill 'im. So help me God, I'll kill 'im!'

They hadn't much to do to control Mano at this stage. His body was supple and weak now, as if his bones were turning to water. The person who had cried, 'It's a damn' shame!' spoke again.
115 'Why you don't carry 'im home, boy? You can't see 'e only making botheration?'

'You'll help me put 'im in the boat?' Sona asked. He looked unruffled now. He seemed only concerned with getting his father out of the shop, and out of all this confusion. Nobody could tell what went on below the calmness of his
120 face. Nobody could guess that hate was blazing in his mind.

Four men and Sona lifted Mano and carted him into the boat. The old man was snoring, in a state of drunkenness. It was the state of drunkenness when things were at rest.

The four men pushed the boat off. Sona looked at his father. After a while he
125 looked back at the bridge. Everything behind was swallowed by the

darkness. 'Pa,' the boy said. His father groaned. 'Pa, yuh going home,' Sona said.

The wilderness of mangroves and river spread out before the boat. They were alone. Sona was alone with Mano, and the river and the mangroves and
130 the night, and the swarms of alligators below. He looked at his father again. 'Pa, so you kick me up then, eh?' he said.

Far into the night Sona's mother waited. She slept a little on one side, then she turned on the other side, and at every sound she woke up, straining her ears. There was no sound of the paddle on water. Surely the shops must have
135 closed by now, she thought. Everything must have closed by this time. She lay there anxious and listened until her eyes shut again in an uneasy sleep.

She was awakened by the creaking of the bedroom floor. Sona jumped back when she spoke.

'Who that – Mano?'
140 'Is me, Ma,' Sona said.

His bones, too, seemed to be turning liquid. Not from drunkenness, but from fear. The lion in him had changed into a lamb. As he spoke his voice trembled.

His mother didn't notice. 'All you now, come?' she said. 'Where Mano?'

The boy didn't answer. In the darkness he took down his things from the
145 nails.

'Where Mano?' his mother cried out.

'He out there sleeping. He drunk.'

'The bitch!' his mother said, getting up and feeling for the matches.

Sona quickly slipped outside. Fear dazed him now and he felt dizzy. He
150 looked at the river and he looked back at the house and there was only one word that kept hitting against his mind: Police!

'Mano!' he heard his mother call to the emptiness of the house. 'Mano!' Panic-stricken, Sona fled into the mangroves and into the night.

Michael Anthony

Understanding

1 The writer's viewpoint plays an important part in the reader's reaction. Shakespeare concentrated on the fearful consequences of the murder for the Macbeths. Dickens condemns Sikes. What is Michael Anthony's attitude towards Sona? Why does he tell us much more than Shakespeare and Dickens about the victim?

Writing

What happened prior to the evening's events? Describe the scene and write the conversation between the three characters on Saturday morning. Keep the characterisation and tension of Michael Anthony's piece.

▭▭▭Ⅲ▷ *LANGUAGE PRACTICE*

Imagery

The purpose of imagery is simple. The writer is saying: 'To give you a clearer idea of what I mean or what I feel, compare this situation with one you are more familiar with.'

If the image begins with a word of comparison, *like* or *as*, it is called a *simile*.
    A *metaphor* is a compressed simile.

FOR EXAMPLE:

    At table he eats *like a pig at its trough*. (simile)
    He is a *pig* at table. (metaphor)

The general term for simile and metaphor is *imagery*.

Brother Leon

The passage about *Brother Leon* on page 20 uses simile to help the reader feel Jerry's response to what is happening.
    Pick out six comparisons and say how they help the reader to understand more clearly or feel more strongly.

FOR EXAMPLE:

    He'd use the tip [of his pointer] to push around a book on a desk or to flick a kid's necktie, scratching gently down some guy's back, poking the pointer as if he were a rubbish collector picking his way through the debris of the classroom.

The simile gives an impression of the way Brother Leon walked round the classroom, actually looking for things to prod, and his feelings about the boys. The whole classroom is debris to him.

Find six other comparisons.

Macbeth

Look at the speech beginning

    Methought I heard . . . on pages 124–125

Here Macbeth builds a series of images about the sleep that he has 'murdered' for himself. What qualities of sleep do the images stress?

Write two lines each about these images in the passage:

    these hangman's hands   (line 20)
    this filthy witness   (line 39)
        The sleeping and the dead
    Are but as pictures.   (lines 45–46)

What hands are here? Ha! They pluck out mine eyes.   (line 51)
   but I shame
To wear a heart so white.   (lines 56–57)

In five lines explain the image about the ocean and the blood on Macbeth's hands.   (lines 51–55)

Imagery – checklist

When judging your own and others' use of imagery remember these points:

1 The image must not be so well-known that its force has been lost
(e.g. *as red as a beetroot*).
2 The image will usually be suitable for more than one reason. For example, comparing Brother Leon with a rubbish collector showed the manner of his parading round the classroom and his feelings about the pupils.
3 The image must be suitable to its subject. (*Her lovely eyes were green as leeks* would create laughter rather than admiration.)
4 The image must make a strong and immediate impression on the senses; if you have to work out what is intended, the force of the image is destroyed.
5 The comparison must be within the reader's experience. (*He looked like my uncle's dog* is going to help very few people.)

Write about this picture for someone who has not seen it. Use vivid imagery.

Variety of language

English has a large variety of words for each concept. *Roget's Thesaurus*, for example, has two full pages on the words connected with the concept of *failure*. The words used below are all taken from those pages; the exercises illustrate their origins, the experiences they have given rise to, and the need to choose the exact word to express your meaning.

Synonyms 1

beating   drubbing   hiding   licking   thrashing   trouncing

These seem to be synonyms, but they are not completely interchangeable because two of them have other meanings. Which two?

Synonyms 2

Study these synonyms for *defeated*:

outclassed   pipped   baffled   routed   thwarted   victimised

Which of these words includes the idea of

a) puzzlement?
b) picked-on unfairly?
c) scattered far and wide?
d) only just beaten?
e) frustrated?
f) easily beaten by a superior opponent?

Metaphors

Where do you think each of these metaphors for *failure* are derived from?

wild-goose chase   misfire   bankrupt   Waterloo   checkmate
flash in the pan   get pipped at the post   go to the dogs   also-ran
draw a blank

Use six of them in sentences of your own to show you understand the metaphorical meaning.

Foreign words

From which European languages have we borrowed these expressions?

faux pas   débâcle   kaput

English has borrowed words from all languages. Match these languages with the list of words below: Italian, Spanish, Greek, German, Latin, Gaelic, French, Arabic.

gondola   décor   siesta   cotton   Sassenach   kudos
ad infinitum   rucksack

Find ten more borrowed words to add to the list. Which language has English borrowed from most?

Colloquialisms

Use each of these colloquial expressions in a sentence to show you understand its meaning.

off day   wash-out   come unstuck   conk out   lose hands down   have not a leg to stand on

━━━▷ *EXAMINATION PRACTICE*

Read this poem and answer the questions on page 140.

The Early Purges

1   I was six when I first saw kittens drown.
Dan Taggart pitched them, 'the scraggy wee pests,'
Into a bucket; a frail metal sound,

   Soft paws scraping like mad. But their tiny din
5 Was soon soused. They were slung on the snout
Of the pump and the water pumped in.

   'Sure isn't it better for them now?' Dan said.
Like wet gloves they bobbed and shone till he sluiced
Them out on the dunghill, glossy and dead.

10 Suddenly frightened, for days I sadly hung
Round the yard, watching the three sogged remains
Turn mealy and crisp as old summer dung

   Until I forgot them. But the fear came back
When Dan trapped big rats, snared rabbits, shot crows
15 Or, with a sickening tug, pulled old hens' necks.

   Still, living displaces false sentiments
And now, when shrill pups are prodded to drown
I just shrug, 'Useless pups'. It makes sense:

   'Prevention of cruelty' talk cuts ice in town
20 Where they consider death unnatural,
But on well-run farms pests have to be kept down.

                  Seamus Heaney

Understanding and directed writing

1 In a passage of 100–150 words explain how the boy's fear and shock is shown through the description of the sights and sounds of the kittens' deaths.
2 What do 'pitched' (line 2), 'slung' (line 5) and 'sluiced' (line 8) show us about Dan? Give a reason for your conclusion by commenting on the choice of words.
3 Choose two comparisons and explain why the poet has used them.
4 In about 30 words say why the poet has or has not made you share the boy's shock at the kittens' death.
5 In the last two verses feelings are replaced by the argument. In about 30 words summarise the argument. Does the argument 'make sense' to you? Give reasons.

8 A sense of place

Places – a valley, a house, a room – are seen differently by different people, or even by the same people at different times or in different moods. Places are therefore a reflection of the people in them.

You are asked to

————————➤ **Distinguish between fact and opinion in an estate agent's advertisement**

————————➤ **Write a report from the buyer's viewpoint**

————————➤ **Distinguish precise from imprecise use of language**

————————➤ **Invent a character to suit particular backgrounds**

————————➤ **Assess different reactions to a particular place**

————————➤ **Write about a place which has special significance for you**

————————➤ **Understand how the atmosphere of a place can be re-created**

————————➤ **Tell or write a supernatural story based on a special place**

————————➤ **Study the use of specialised vocabulary**

Examination practice – continuous writing

Small's Estate Agent

PRIMROSE COTTAGE, SURTON.
PRICE: £45,000

This charming cottage needs to be
seen to be believed. A unique
opportunity to acquire a splendid
property in this select area.
At present some modernisation and
updating is required to enhance
its immense charm and potential.
Surton is a much sought-after
village with its own primary
school and shopping area.

The accommodation comprises

<u>Lounge</u> - a truly superb room of immense character: exposed beams. Large
walk-round fireplace. Charming brick chimney breast. In good decorative
order.

<u>Kitchen</u> - a large room which could easily be transformed into a modern
fitted kitchen. Open fire. Electric points. Needs some attention to
wiring.

<u>Dining-room</u> - a delightful room with large windows overlooking the rear
garden. Needs some attention to decoration. Large open fire.

<u>Hall</u> - large, attractive wooden staircase leading to:

<u>Landing</u> - ornamental rose to ceiling.

<u>Bedroom</u> 1 - large, airy room, exposed beams. Window overlooking rural
aspect.

<u>Bedroom</u> 2 - large room. Window overlooking farmland.

<u>Bedroom</u> 3 - smaller than bedrooms 1 and 2. Ideal size for a guest room.

No electrical points at present on first floor.

Bathroom - spacious. Room for double bath and bidet. At present in need
of some renovation. Water heated from back boiler in kitchen.

Outside - space at rear for two cars. Small well-stocked gardens.

The purpose of the description

The purpose of this description is to attract buyers. Divide the information given into three categories:

1 *The facts*. What you know for certain about the house, for instance the number of rooms.
2 The descriptive words or phrases that are *matters of opinion*, for instance 'a truly superb room of immense character'.
3 References that are *not sufficiently defined*, for example '*some* renovation'.

Write a paragraph on each of the three categories.

A report

You have been asked to look at the house on behalf of a buyer. Write a 100-word report, based on the estate agent's description, setting out the advantages and disadvantages of the house in a precise and factual manner.

You will need, therefore, to concentrate on the *facts* and ignore the *matters of opinion*.

Organise your report in the way that the estate agent has by taking each room in turn. Conclude with your overall recommendation to the buyer.

Vocabulary

The language of the description is extravagant and imprecise. For instance, in everyday language *to buy* is preferable to the pompous *to acquire*, and in the sentence *At present . . . is required* the phrase *at present* is unnecessary.

Choose the word you prefer from each pair below. For three examples say when and why you might use the alternative.

about/approximately	buy/purchase	endeavour/try
category/class	meet/encounter	help/assist
vocalist/singer	dentures/false teeth	begin/commence
erect/build	enquire/ask	donate/give

Writing

Compose an estate agent's description of your house or flat. Remember the purpose – 'to attract buyers'. What features will you emphasise and what faults will you try to disguise?

PLACE AS SETTING FOR CHARACTER

Wuthering Heights

Lockwood is escaping town life by renting an old manor house in Yorkshire for the summer. He visits his landlord, a strange man called Heathcliff, at the neighbouring farm 'Wuthering Heights'.

1   Wuthering Heights is the name of Mr Heathcliff's dwelling. 'Wuthering' being a Yorkshire adjective, descriptive of the wind to which it is exposed in stormy weather. Pure, bracing air they must have up there at all times, indeed: one may guess the power of the north wind, blowing over the edge, by the
5   excessive slant of a few stunted firs at the end of the house; and by a range of gaunt thorns all stretching their limbs one way, as if craving the sun. Luckily the architect had foresight to build it strong: the narrow windows are deeply set in the wall, and the corners defended with large jutting stones.

Before entering, I paused to admire a quantity of grotesque carving over the
10 front, and especially about the principal door, above which, among a wilderness of crumbling griffins, and shameless little boys, I detected the date '1500' and the name 'Hareton Earnshaw'. I would have made a few comments and requested a short history of the place from the surly owner, but his attitude at the door appeared to demand my speedy entrance, or complete
15 departure, and I had no desire to aggravate his impatience.

One step brought us into the family sitting-room, without any introductory lobby, or passage: they call it here 'the house'. It includes kitchen, and parlour, generally, but I believe at Wuthering Heights the kitchen is forced to retreat altogether into another quarter, at least I distinguished a chatter of
20 tongues, and a clatter of pots deep within; and I observed no signs of roasting, boiling, or baking, about the huge fire-place; nor any glitter of copper saucepans and tin cullenders on the walls. One end, indeed, reflected splendidly both light and heat, from ranks of immense pewter dishes, and silver jugs and tankards, towering row after row, in a vast oak dresser, to the
25 very roof. The beams were exposed except where a frame of wood laden with oatcakes, and clusters of legs of beef, mutton, and ham concealed them. Above the chimney were various villainous old guns, and a couple of horse-pistols, and, by way of ornament, three gaudily painted canisters along its ledge. The floor was of smooth, white stone: the chairs, high-backed, wooden,
30 primitive structures, painted green: one or two heavy black ones lurking in the shade. In an arch under the dresser lay a huge, liver-coloured bitch pointer surrounded by a swarm of squealing puppies.

Emily Brontë

Understanding the passage

1 Imagine that 'Wuthering Heights' is for sale. Write the estate agent's description of the outside and the parlour.
2 Heathcliff is described as *surly* and is unwelcoming. How is 'Wuthering Heights' a good setting for such a character?

Characters and their houses

1 What kinds of people might live in these houses? Choose one and write about a visit you made.

2 Imagine and make notes about the houses that each of these characters might live in:

a jolly person, who likes cats, reading crime stories and eating chocolates

a suspicious person, who rarely goes out and who is suspected of hoarding a great deal of money

a friendly outgoing person who is always having parties and entertaining people

a nervous shy person, who would like to be friendly but is actually very lonely

Write about a visit you made to *one* of these people and describe the person in his/her setting.

A CLASSROOM

Three people describe a classroom from their own point of view.

The cleaner showing a new cleaner what to do

'Phoo! Stuffy in here, isn't it? All those bodies! I never understand why they keep those curtains shut once the sun's moved round. Makes the place so gloomy. I'll just open them. See, there's cords at either end to open them. Now, all we've got to do is move all the desks and chairs to the side of the room. The chairs will stack which saves a lot of space. They're not too heavy those desks – you can stack them too. Then we just empty the bin and sweep the floor. I know it looks a bit scruffy, but we're only supposed to polish it once every half-term. We'll have to move quick because there's a dance class coming in soon. Found some chewing-gum under the desk, have you? Ooh, they are a dirty lot.'

A new student's view

'This desk wobbles. I wonder if it would be all right if I put a piece of paper under one of the legs. The floor's in a bad way – all scuffed and scratched. Years of scraping chairs and scuffling feet, I suppose. I'd better get on with my work – the teacher's just stood up from her desk to have a walk round. I wish she'd shut those curtains. The sun's right in my eyes. The view's not wonderful anyway – just a lot of cars and houses. That notice-board could do with a new look too. The posters are all curled up at the edges. No, there's not much of interest to take your attention away from work.'

The teacher reports on the condition of her room

'The walls were painted only a year ago. It's a pretty hideous institution green but you have to put up with the colour you are given. The floor is badly scuffed – I do think it ought to be polished more often. It isn't a bad room to work in. The windows are nice and big and you can see right over the car-park and into town. You can even see the river if you are standing at the front of the class. I know I ought to change my display more often – those posters are two years old and going brown and curly at the edges. There's lots of space and the desks are light so you can move them around if you want to. The children will keep sticking chewing-gum underneath the desks – I have to have a regular session to clear it up.'

Summary

Using all three accounts, make a list of the *facts* about the room.

Writing

Make a list of details about your own classroom. Write descriptions of the room from these points of view:

the cleaner
a student
the teacher

A PLACE IN YOUR AFFECTIONS

Read this extract from *Michael* by William Wordsworth.

Michael is a Westmorland shepherd; the mountains and valleys are not simply pleasant surroundings but an important part of the shepherd's life, a record book in which every part of the surroundings reminds him of some incident.

Michael

1   And grossly that man errs, who should suppose
    That the green valleys, and the streams and rocks,
    Were things indifferent to the Shepherd's thoughts.
    Fields, where with cheerful spirits he had breathed
5   The common air; hills, which with vigorous step
    He had so often climbed; which had impressed
    So many incidents upon his mind
    Of hardship, skill or courage, joy or fear;
    Which, like a book, preserved the memory
10 Of the dumb animals, whom he had saved,
    Had fed or sheltered, linking to such acts
    The certainty of honourable gain;
    Those fields, those hills – what could they less – had laid
    Strong hold on his affections, were to him
15 A pleasurable feeling of blind love,
    The pleasure which there is in life itself.

William Wordsworth

Writing

Write about a place that has a strong hold on your affections. Notice that not all the shepherd's memories are happy ones. The poet refers to incidents of

   hardship, skill or courage, joy or fear

but they all contribute to the feeling that the place is part of the person.

CREATING AN ATMOSPHERE

Wuthering Heights

A bad snowstorm prevents Lockwood from leaving 'Wuthering Heights'. He is forced to stay the night. The servant girl, Zillah, shows him to his room.

1   While leading the way upstairs, Zillah recommended that I should hide the candle, and not make a noise, for her master had an odd notion about the chamber she would put me in; and never let anybody lodge there willingly.
    I asked the reason.
5   She did not know, she answered; she had only lived there a year or two; and they had so many queer goings on, she could not begin to be curious.
    Too stupefied myself, I fastened my door and glanced round for the bed. The whole furniture consisted of a chair, a clothes cupboard and a large oak case, with squares cut out near the top, resembling coach windows.
10   Having approached this structure, I looked inside, and perceived it to be an odd sort of old-fashioned bed. It formed a little closet, and the ledge of a window, which it enclosed, served as a table.
    I slid back the panelled sides, got in with my light, pulled them together again, and felt secure against the vigilance of Heathcliff, and every one else.
15   The ledge where I placed my candle had a few mildewed books piled up in one corner; and it was covered with writing scratched on the paint. This writing, however, was nothing but a name repeated in all kinds of characters, large and small – Catherine Earnshaw; here and there varied to Catherine Heathcliff, and then again to Catherine Linton.
20   Idly I leant my head against the window, and continued spelling over Catherine Earnshaw – Heathcliff – Linton, till my eyes closed.
    I began to dream. I thought it was morning; and I had set out on my way home. The snow lay yards deep and I floundered about, lost. All landmarks had disappeared. I did not even know if I was still on the road. Suddenly there
25 was a tremendous tumult and I disappeared under an avalanche of snow. To my unspeakable relief, I woke up.
    And what was it that had suggested the tremendous tumult? Merely the branch of a fir-tree that touched my window, as the blast wailed by, and rattled its dry cones against the panes!
30   I listened doubtingly an instant; realised what had woken me, then turned and dozed, and dreamt again; if possible, still more disagreeably than before.
    This time, I remembered I was lying in the oak closet, and I heard distinctly the gusty wind, and the driving of the snow; I heard also, the fir-bough repeat its teasing sound, but it annoyed me so much, that I resolved to silence it, if
35 possible; and, I thought, I rose and tried to open the window. The hook was soldered into the staple, a circumstance observed by me when awake, but forgotten.

'I must stop it, nevertheless!' I muttered, knocking my knuckles through the glass, and stretching an arm out to seize the offending branch: instead of
40 which, my fingers closed on the fingers of a little, ice-cold hand!
The intense horror of the nightmare came over me; I tried to draw back my arm, but the hand clung to it, and a most melancholy voice sobbed,
'Let me in – let me in!'
'Who are you?' I asked, struggling, meanwhile, to disengage myself.
45 'Catherine Linton,' it replied shiveringly. 'I'm come home, I'd lost my way on the moor!'
As it spoke, I could just see a child's face looking through the window – terror made me cruel; and, finding it useless to attempt shaking the creature off, I pulled its wrist on to the broken pane, and rubbed it to and fro till the
50 blood ran down and soaked the bedclothes: still it wailed, 'Let me in!' and maintained its tenacious grip, almost maddening me with fear.
'How can I?' I said at length. 'Let *me* go, if you want me to let you in!'
The fingers relaxed, I snatched mine through the hole, hurriedly piled the books up in a pyramid against it, and stopped my ears against the lamentable
55 prayer.
I seemed to keep them closed above a quarter of an hour, yet, the instant I listened again, there was the doleful cry moaning on!
'Begone!' I shouted, 'I'll never let you in, not if you beg for twenty years.'
'It's twenty years,' mourned the voice, 'twenty years, I've been a waif for
60 twenty years!'
Thereat began a feeble scratching outside, and the pile of books moved as if thrust forward.
I tried to jump up, but could not stir a limb; and so yelled aloud, in a frenzy of fright.

Emily Brontë
(slightly abridged and adapted)

Drawing conclusions

1 What evidence is there that the story takes place a long time ago?
2 How are we prepared for the fact that something strange might happen?

Convincing the reader

Many people do not believe in ghosts. Others need to be persuaded to accept a ghost story. Emily Brontë makes her story convincing, by giving us a setting, the details of which we can see, and by making the ghost as vivid as possible.

1 We usually imagine ghosts to be transparent and insubstantial. What makes the ghost of Catherine so horrifying?
2 Write a description of the room in as much detail as you can.

Creating suspense

Emily Brontë intended this account of Lockwood's nightmare to arouse your curiosity so that you would want to read on. Test whether she has succeeded by writing down a list of questions which the passage arouses in you.

Oral work

Tell a ghost story that you know. Decide which stories sound the most interesting and convincing, and why.

Writing

Write down your ghost story. Make it sound as convincing as possible by giving it a setting, the details of which your reader can see clearly. Try to avoid the clichés of ghost stories – old castles, chains, disembodied heads.

 LANGUAGE PRACTICE

Dialects

If language is to convey meaning precisely, we must have not only a common understanding of what each word means, but also a common understanding of how each word is written.

However, we do not all speak in the same way. Someone from Liverpool sounds very different from someone from Glasgow. We say that they speak with different *accents*. Some TV announcers have quite strong accents. Sometimes people in one part of the country also have different words for some things, or use a slightly different form of grammar when they speak. When this happens, we say that they are speaking in *dialect*. Usually, of course, if people are speaking in, for example, a Dorset dialect, they will also speak with a Dorset accent. Writers sometimes try to convey in written form the sound and manner of a particular dialect.

Read these five representations of different regional speech.

1 'Well,' says Ma, 'I kind of had my face for chicken but I guess we c'n manage. Here, Lump, you run down to Perkins' grocery and fetch up a few cans salmon an' any other vittles ye might think of.'

'Not me,' Lump says, 'Gedge tole me if I got caught swipin' any more stuff out'n stores, he'd send me to state's prison sure 'nough.'

(*The Jukes Family* by Frank Sullivan)

151

2 'Here, I browt thee a bit o' brandysnap, an' a coconut for th' children. It's a good 'un, you may back yer life o' that. I got it fra' Bill. "Bill," I says, "tha non wants them three nuts, does ter? Arenter for gi'ein' me one for my bit of a lad an' wench?" "I ham, Walter, my lad," 'e says; "ta'e which on 'em ter's a mind."' (*Sons and Lovers* by D H Lawrence)

3 'She do belong to that class of womankind that become zecond wives: a rum class rather. You zee her first husband was a young man who let her go too far; in fact, she used to kick up Bob's-a-dying at the least thing in the world. And when I'd married her and found it out, I thought, thinks I, "'Tis too late now to begin to cure 'ee," and so I let her bide. Wives be such a provoking class of society because, though they never be right, they never be more than half wrong.' (*Under the Greenwood Tree* by Thomas Hardy)

4 'Nah Jooab's middlin' thick like, bur'e'd a 'ad to be a deal thicker net ta know ut there wer summat wrang t'way ut shoo were preychin' on, an' so 'e let paper tummle outnt' flooar an 'e sat theer an' gasped woll shoo stopped fer breath, an' then 'e sez, "What the heck 'as ta agate on, lass? Is there summat up or summat?" An' that didn't mend matters one iota. All it did wer ta start 'er off ageean.' (*Runnin' Repairs* by G Vine)

5 'What have you been doing?' asked the doctor.
   'Nothink, sir. Never done nothink to get myself into trouble 'sept not moving on. But I'm a-moving on now – on to the berryin ground – that's the move as I'm up to.'
   'What did the man do to you?'
   'Put me in a horsepittle,' replied Jo, 'then giv me a little money and ses "Hook it! Move on!" he ses. "Don't ever let me see you nowheres." He was hard upon me.' (*Bleak House* by Charles Dickens)

Understanding

1 Pair off each passage with its dialect:

Cockney
West Country (Dorset)
Yorkshire
America
Midlands (Derbyshire)

2 Give reasons for your choice.

3 The grammar of dialect may differ from standard grammar. What is the standard English equivalent of the underlined words?

she <u>do</u> belong	there <u>wer</u> summat wrang
to cure <u>'ee</u>	shoo <u>were</u> preychin' on
wives <u>be</u> such a provoking class	<u>never done nothink</u>

4 Dialect is as much a matter of expression as of sound. Put each of these expressions into a standard English form.

I kind of had my face for chicken
ta'e which on 'em ter's a mind
she used to kick up Bob's-a-dying
Nah Jooab's middlin' thick like
that's the move as I'm up to

Oral work

Choose one of the passages and practise speaking it in dialect. Perform it to the rest of your class.

Writing

Try writing a piece of any dialect you are familiar with. Are there any words unique to your dialect? Are there any variations from standard grammar, particularly with the verb *to be*?

▭▥▷ *EXAMINATION PRACTICE*

Continuous writing

Write on *one* of the subjects below. You may include a plan to help you construct and organise your writing.

You should write between 300 and 500 words. You may make up the material or use your own experiences, or employ a combination of both. Be careful to check that you have written paragraphs and that your full stops and spelling are correct.

1 **A day to remember**
The day may have pleasant or unpleasant memories. Do not simply tell the story of the day's events; include your thoughts and feelings.

2 **Work experience**
Give an account of a period you have spent on work experience and assess its value to you.

3 **Irritations**
Write about some of the things that annoy you. You may, if you wish, concentrate on one thing, but do not tell a story. Explain the sources of your irritation, your feelings and your reactions.

4 Write about the photograph below.

Your writing may be directly about the subject of the picture, or may take only some suggestions from it, but there must be a clear connection between your writing and the photograph.

9 Specialised language

The language of the law

This section studies how a specialised form of language and procedure is adopted for a particular purpose – the law.

You are asked to

————————→ Read three scenes from a trial

————————→ Understand the purpose of the legal method

————————→ Analyse the purpose of the vocabulary and style

————————→ Write further scenes from the trial in the appropriate language

————————→ Discuss the fairness of the legal system

————————→ Understand and write satirical pieces on the law

————————→ Study closely the language of the law

————————→ Look at the language used by four people to describe their special interests

Examination practice – use a newspaper report as a basis for directed writing

Your witness – scenes from a trial

John Edgar is charged with

1 Breaking open 19 post boxes
2 Stealing the mail from the boxes
3 Attempting to cash cheques stolen from the mail.

These three scenes are from John Edgar's trial.
   Six people are involved:

Counsel for the prosecution	— tries to prove that John Edgar is guilty
Counsel for the defence	— tries to prove that John Edgar is not guilty
The judge	— controls the proceedings
Alison Coton	— a witness for the prosecution
Mrs Hayes	— a witness for the defence
Sergeant Jacobs	— a police witness

There are twelve members of the jury, but they do not speak.

The three scenes are from various parts of the trial. Before the first one the prosecuting counsel has described how the post boxes were opened (with an iron bar) and when and where the robberies took place.

Scene 1

The prosecuting counsel is questioning Sergeant Jacobs.

S.J. (*reading from a notebook*)   1
I interviewed Mr Edgar at 43, Maltby Crescent at 9.05 a.m. on October
14th 1986. I cautioned him . . .
P.C. What did you say to him?
S.J. I said to him, 'You are not obliged to say anything, but anything you   5
say may be written down and used in evidence against you.'
P.C. And you made notes of your conversation?
S.J. Yes.
P.C. Did you make your notes during the interview?
S.J. My notes were not made contemporaneously, but immediately   10
following the interview.
P.C. So the conversation was fresh in your mind?
S.J. Yes.
P.C. Please read your account.
S.J. I informed Mr Edgar that he was to be charged in connection with   15
breaking into nineteen post boxes in the Danderson area, stealing
an unknown quantity of mail and attempting to obtain monies by
fraudulent means with cheques known to be stolen. He replied, 'You
have got to be joking. Do my arms look long and thin enough to reach

John Edgar

Sergeant Jacobs

Alison Coton

Mrs Hayes

down a post box slit?' I warned him that the matter in question was a   20
serious one. He replied, 'It will be for you, if you can't prove it.' I then
showed him a cheque.

P.C. Exhibit B, your Honour.

Judge Have the jury copies?   25

P.C. Yes, your Honour. As the jury can see, Your Honour, the cheque
appears to be made out to C.O. Hector from the firm of Godson and
Drury for seven thousand, nine hundred pounds. Later I will
produce evidence to show that the cheque was originally made
payable to Collector of Taxes and that 'of Taxes' has been   30
obliterated. Also, full stops have been inserted after the 'C' and 'O'
of Collector and the two 'l's' have been crossed to form the capital
'H' of 'Hector'. Carry on, Sergeant.

S.J. I asked Mr Edgar if he had seen the cheque. He replied that he had
not. I then asked him how he explained that his fingerprints had   35
been found on it. He then looked at the cheque again and said, 'Oh
yes, it's the one I put in a bank for a bloke I met at a party.'
  I asked Mr Edgar if he had opened an account at the Midland
Bank in Angel Street in the name of Carl Hector. He replied, 'No way.
Look, I had my suspicions that the cheque was a bit dodgy, but all I'm   40
admitting is that I put it in the bank for this bloke.'

P.C. Did you ask the defendant if he knew the name of this person?

S.J. Yes. He said, 'I only met him once. His name was Carl. I don't know his
other name. He's gone up North, I reckon.'

Scene 2

*The prosecuting counsel is questioning Alison Coton. Mrs Coton is an old lady
who lives in the Danderson area where the post boxes were broken into. She has
already explained how she was woken at 2 a.m. by the squealing of tyres and a
crashing noise. She looked out of her window.*

P.C. Please describe what you saw.   1

Alison A car had drawn up sort of sideways, half of it on the pavement.
It had hit my dustbin. I've had that dustbin for . . .

P.C. Were there any people in the car?

Alison Two I think. One was outside. He had a bar thing in his hand.   5
Then I heard him shout, 'John, John over here,' and I saw this other
man running to the car. He was carrying a bag, one like you'd get
out of Tesco's and he had a bar thing as well.

P.C. What happened then?

Alison They both just jumped in the car and it drove off very fast.   10

P.C. Did you hear anything else?

Alison The tyres squealed and . . .

P.C. Was another name mentioned?

Alison Oh, yes, I forgot. The man who came running said, 'Is that you, Pete?'   15

P.C. Did you notice anything about the car?

Alison It was blue. It was like my son's. It was a Ford.
   P.C. A Cortina?
   D.C. Objection. My Lord, this is the second occasion my learned friend
        has led the witness.   20
Judge Re-phrase the question.
   P.C. What kind of car was it?
Alison A Cortina like my son's. It had those funny wheels.
   P.C. Would you describe them in more detail?

Scene 3

*The defence counsel is finishing his questioning of Mrs Hayes, John Edgar's
landlady.*

   D.C. How do you remember so clearly that Mr Edgar stayed in the   1
        night on which the robberies took place?
Mrs H. Because it was my birthday.
   D.C. Did Mr Edgar join in your birthday celebration?
Mrs H. He came and had a drink with me. About 9 o'clock. Then he went   5
        back to his room.
   D.C. And he didn't go out again that night?
Mrs H. No, I'd have heard him. You can hear the stairs creaking.
        (*D.C. sits down*)
   P.C. Mrs Hayes, I believe Mr Edgar's brother is a tenant of yours?   10
Mrs H. That's right.

P.C. And his name?

Mrs H. Well, Mr Edgar, of course.

P.C. No, his Christian name.

Mrs H. It's Peter, I think.   15

P.C. You know it's Peter, Mrs Hayes.

Mrs H. Yes, it's Peter.

P.C. Mrs Hayes, I believe Mr Edgar owns a car.

Mrs H. Yes. He parks it in the drive.

P.C. What kind of car?   20

Mrs H. Oh, I don't know about cars.

P.C. Is it blue?

Mrs H. Yes.

P.C. Is it a Cortina, Mrs Hayes?

Mrs H. Yes, I think it is.   25

P.C. Now, Mrs Hayes. Would it be possible for someone to come down your stairs without making a creak?

Mrs H. Well, you'd have to be very careful and I don't . . .

P.C. Thank you, Mrs Hayes.

Understanding

Scene 1

In a short paragraph explain why and in what way the criminal had altered the cheque and how he intended to use it.

Two facts you need to know:

1 You can open a bank account by depositing £1.
2 You have to pay a cheque into an account before you can withdraw the money.

Scene 2

What are the important facts the prosecuting counsel gets from Alison Coton?

Scene 3

What is Mrs Hayes trying to establish for John Edgar?
What important information does the prosecuting counsel get from her?

Drawing conclusions

Scene 1

What is the prosecuting counsel trying to establish before the Sergeant reads his account?
Why are John Edgar's comments always in inverted commas?

Scene 2

What does the defence counsel mean when he says the witness is being led? (Look at the re-phrasing of the question.)

Scene 3

What details does Mrs Hayes seem reluctant to admit? Why?
Why does the lawyer stop her finishing her last remark?

Vocabulary and style

Vocabulary

Re-read the caution given to John Edgar by the Sergeant. Compare it with this version: 'You don't have to talk to me, but if you do I'll write down what you say and perhaps use it to try to get you convicted.' What is the difference? Which version do you prefer?
Find phrases or words from the Sergeant's and the counsels' speeches that could be written either more simply or more colloquially.

Whose manner of expression contrasts vividly with those of the Sergeant and the counsels?

Style

There is a distinct form in which evidence is given and witnesses questioned. In pairs practise the form by questioning each other about some simple matter – what you did last night or what happened in Maths. You need to consider your questions carefully. For example you would ask 'What time did you arrive at the lesson?' not 'Did you arrive late for the lesson?' When you have finished decide the purpose of this method of questioning.

Writing

Scene 1

Add the defence counsel's questioning of Sergeant Jacobs. Imagine that John Edgar has told his counsel:
1 That he told the Sergeant he admitted seeing the cheque before he was told

his fingerprints were on it. (Why would this be important if true?)
2 The Sergeant told him that three other cheques had been found with his fingerprints on them. This had turned out to be untrue. Invent other questions to help John Edgar. The cheque would have other fingerprints on it, for instance. Has the Sergeant any evidence to show John's story is untrue?

Scene 2

Write the defence counsel's questioning of Alison Coton. He or she will be trying to cast doubt on Alison's evidence.

A longer project

Complete the whole case:
1 Write the dialogue of questions and answers between the judge and John Edgar.
2 With a friend, role-play the questioning.
3 Continue the dialogue with the judge's summing-up and the jury's discussion and verdict. Remember that no evidence has yet been shown to connect John Edgar beyond doubt with the robberies themselves.

Discussion

1 The atmosphere in a Crown Court is formal. The lawyers wear wigs and black gowns. They address each other as *my learned friend* and call the judge *your Honour.*

   Everyone stands when the judge enters and leaves. Give other examples of the formality of the court, discuss their purpose and decide whether a more relaxed atmosphere would be better or worse.

2 'There is no fairer way of arriving at the truth than the jury system, which allows twelve people chosen at random to make judgment.'
   Discuss this statement.
   Only criminals, lunatics and Members of Parliament are barred from jury service. Would you make other exceptions?

▭▭▷ *LANGUAGE PRACTICE*

Vocabulary

There are over half a million words in the English Language. Each of us knows only a limited number of these and uses even less. But the more words we recognise, the better we are able to understand and enjoy our world.

Each special area of knowledge has its own specialised vocabulary. Here are four people writing about their own special interest:

> Photographs can be taken in moonlight, but exposure time, as compared with that in daylight, will have to be increased by at least a hundred thousand times – say 15 minutes at f/5.6 at full moon. Neither the moon nor its reflection in water can be included in the field of view. Light from a half-moon will not, surprisingly enough, require double the exposure time of that from a full moon but will have to be increased five times. Shorter exposures are, of course, possible with a wider aperture and even snapshots are sometimes possible given a fast lens, fast film, and strong artificial light such as that from a shop window.

> Glaucoma, an eye disease associated with a rise in tension inside the eye, is responsible for the blindness of one in seven of the registered blind. Forty per cent of those who go blind from glaucoma have not been diagnosed and treated for the condition until they have become blind, for symptoms can be very late in appearing. Early detection, therefore, is sight-saving, and screening of whole populations, particularly of the age chiefly at risk, has been introduced in Britain.

> Deal with a skid caused by hard breaking by steering straight or as straight as possible instantly. Turned steering encourages brake locking and throws you off course. In the fastest possible stop, wheels at no time lock but are held at the point of locking throughout. The retarding effect utterly depends on tyre grip against the surface. The constant supply of fresh tread maintained by keeping the wheel rolling is what matters.
>
> Directly a wheel locks, one small pad of tread has all the work to do and there is no hope of retarding as effectively. This tiny area of tread abruptly finds itself scraping along the abrasive surface leaving a trail of skin rubber. It heats rapidly, and may even start to melt.

Camel's meat has been regarded with favour since the time of the ancient Greeks. The Arabs eat camels when they are young and the meat is tender. The hump, the feet and the stomach are the parts most appreciated by connoisseurs.

To prepare the fillet of a young animal, marinate with oil, lemon juice, salt, pepper and spices and roast on a spit.

For camel ribs with rice, trim the camel ribs and marinate. Sauté them in butter or oil. Drain them of fat and set them on a round dish. Garnish with a rice pilaf. Dress with a sauce made with the juices remaining in the pan to which a few tablespoons of stock and a little seasoning have been added.

A word for every occasion

1 What is the subject matter of each writer?
2 Summarise in one or two sentences what point each writer is making.
3 Make lists of the specialised vocabulary which each writer uses. Say what each word means. (If you do not know, or cannot guess from the context, use a dictionary.)

Your own special interest

Write 200 words on your own hobby, interest or field of knowledge. At the end of your piece, make a vocabulary list, explaining the meaning of the words which you think will be unfamiliar to those who do not share your interest.

▭▭▭▭▶ *EXAMINATION PRACTICE*

Read this newspaper article on children's health.

Children 'healthier 35 years ago'

by David Henke, Social Services Correspondent

Children today are more likely to be admitted to hospital or suffer from asthma, eczema and diabetes than their parents born and brought up in the austerity years* after the second world war.

Findings by the Medical Research Council to be released today at the annual British Society for Population Studies conference at Sussex University will show that in some cases children's health is worse now than it was 35 years ago.

A paper* by Dr Michael Wadsworth, deputy chairman of the MRC's National Survey of Health and Development at Bristol University, compares the health of over 5,000 people born in 1946 and their first-born children a generation later.

The survey found substantial increases in the hospital admission of children up to the age of four, a tripling of instances of asthma, and a six-fold increase in eczema among the new generation. There was a substantial reduction in cases of children losing tonsils or adenoids, and a big reduction in ear infections.

Hospital admissions for suspected accidental injuries rose by nearly 50 per cent. Part of the reason for this is that doctors detained people overnight to check for hidden injuries. But the survey also found that child minders, and teachers made more use of the hospital services to ensure that children had no broken bones.

Cases of eczema rose from 2.2 per 1,000 first-born in 1946 to 12.3 per 1,000 in the succeeding generation. One reason might be that doctors spotted the disease, the other that increased use of agricultural chemicals, household detergents and soap are responsible.

Asthma increased from 6.2 per 1,000 to 18.9 per 1,000 between generations – increased pollution could be responsible.

Juvenile diabetes rose nearly six-fold between the generations, perhaps caused by the ability of children who are disposed to diabetes to survive more easily in the 1970s and 1980s.

Obesity also has doubled for boys and nearly doubled for girls during the same period.*

Other points raised by the research include the rising divorce and separation rate in modern marriages. This is seen to cause emotional problems for children.

Dr Wadsworth, a social scientist, warns that it will be difficult to draw firm conclusions from the study.

He said yesterday: 'The problem is that present monitoring is totally useless. We are good at following birth and death statistics but not in monitoring children's health.'

He is calling for a national monitoring system based on a sample of 6,000 to 7,000 children to be set up by the Government. 'Information for such an investigation should be collected by nurses at annual home visits at approximately the time of the child's birthday. If repeated on a new child population after a period of five years this study would provide information about change in child health and the experience of illness, and begin what could become a process of monitoring.'

*austerity years – years of comparative poverty
*paper – document
*Obesity etc. Today twice as many boys and almost twice as many girls are overweight compared with figures 35 years ago.

Directed writing – a report

Set out in note form the facts about the increase in reported cases of asthma, eczema and diabetes and the increased number of hospital admissions.

   Write a report of two paragraphs, each of about a hundred words. Use only information from the passage.

Begin the first paragraph:

'There is certainly some cause for concern in the figures . . .'

Begin the second paragraph:

'There are, however, other possible explanations that will cause no alarm.'

Designing a poster

Design a poster to encourage children to eat fewer sweets. Use information from the article, but add some of your own ideas if you wish.

10 Making a choice

This section deals with assessing evidence and making reasoned choices.

You are asked to

⟶ Use a *Which?* guide to choose places to eat for different people

⟶ Write a local *Which?* report

⟶ Choose a holiday from a *Which?* report

⟶ Compare the *Which?* report with an advertisement

⟶ Examine how a writer's purpose influences both the content and language of a description

⟶ Study closely the language of newspapers

Examination practice – make notes on holiday advertisements and design one yourself

Wimpy
Branches 545, throughout UK
Opening times Every day, between 10 a.m. and 10 p.m. – precise times vary between branches
Price of our selected meal £1.15 to £1.40
Licensed Very few branches
Service Waiter or counter and take-away
Provisions for children Comics, badges, special menu, high chairs at some branches
No-smoking area None
Comments Reports didn't agree about the food, although 'fair and satisfactory quality' was a more typical comment than hamburgers 'flannelly and tasteless'. Of those who mentioned price, over half thought the chain expensive. We had more reports of quick service (to the point of being rushed) than complaints of it being slow, although 'a definite lack of friendliness' had been experienced by several members. Generally Wimpys were described as clean, but several reports said they were cramped. Overall not wildly praised, but good for a quick snack.

Pizzaland
Branches 65, throughout UK
Opening times Every day, 9.30 a.m. to 11.30 p.m. (midnight at some London branches)
Price of our selected meal £1.70
Licensed Yes
Service Waiter and take-away
Provisions for children No special menu, but pizza slices served; booster seats at some branches
No-smoking area Some branches
Comments Opinions differed on the pizzas – some held they were good value, others found them, and the baked potatoes, disappointing. 'The service varies enormously from fast, to slow and incorrect' – the variation seemed to be between branches, and according to how busy the restaurant was. Almost half the reports mentioned 'seating rather crammed together', but some also noted the clean, bright restaurant interiors. Despite some criticism, several reports concluded that the chain offered value for money.

Burger House
Branches 36, throughout England
Opening times Every day, between 8 a.m. and 11 p.m. – precise times vary between branches
Price of our selected meal £1.11 to £1.28
Licensed 2 branches only
Service Waiter (but counter only at 2 branches) and take-away
Provisions for children Children's menu
No-smoking area Some branches
Comments 'Good choice on menu' began one report, but then continued with 'prices rather high for what you get'. We didn't get enough reports to tell you how the interiors look generally, or if service tends to be slow or quick or friendly, but all reports said the restaurants were clean.

Happy Eater
Branches 18, throughout England
Opening times Every day, 8 a.m. to 8 p.m., some branches open for longer
Price of our selected meal £2.05
Licensed Yes
Service Waiter and take-away for some items
Provisions for children Special menu, high chairs and booster seats, play areas at some branches, badges, lollipops and toothbrushes given away, birthday club and parties; Happy Eater shop; will heat your baby food or supply boiled water or hot milk
No-smoking area Yes
Comments 'We were very favourably impressed on all counts.' With a few exceptions, most people thought the food and service good. Restaurants were clean, and often thought pleasant and 'certainly geared to the needs of children'. Overall – good places for the motorist who wants a simple and not too expensive meal.

Little Chef
Branches 188, throughout Great Britain
Opening times Every day, 8 a.m. to 8 p.m. – some branches open for longer, up to 24 hours
Price of our selected meal £2.45
Licensed No
Service Waiter
Provisions for children Special menu, high chairs, seat raisers, lollipop for finishing meal
No-smoking area None
Comments Several reports referred to the popularity of Little Chefs which sometimes led to them being overcrowded. With a few exceptions, the general opinion was 'quality and value not only good, but consistent'. Service usually quick and friendly, but could be slow when busy. Restaurants were clean, but tables sometimes thought a bit small. Children well-catered for. A few branches had proved disappointing, but a frequent comment was 'an excellent place to break a journey'.

McDonald's
Branches 53, South-East and Midlands
Opening times Every day, 10 a.m. to 11 p.m.
Price of our selected meal £1.10
Licensed No
Service Counter and take-away
Provisions for children High chairs, toddler seats, badges, hats, and parties catered for
No-smoking area None
Comments Most reports praised the food – 'excellent provided you like that type of food' – if you don't mind eating with your fingers. But a few felt that it was 'pre-fabricated and unappetising'. Most thought the prices reasonable, although a few found the chain pricey. 'The service is very fast, except at peak times' – and several reports referred to long waits for burgers without relish. Impressive cleanliness, but a few people complained of 'not very comfortable seating'. Several reports praised the welcoming attitude to children. Overall – fine for a quick snack, if you can avoid the most popular times.

CHOOSING A PLACE TO EAT

Write a report

Study the information given about these six fast-food chain restaurants and write reports for two of the groups of people below advising them where to eat.

1 A family with two children travelling by car looking for a cheap place with quick service which caters for young children. One child is allergic to cigarette smoke.

2 Two teenagers stopping in town looking for a cheerful but cheap place for lunch.

3 Parents looking for a place where their son aged 12 can take his friend for a birthday meal. Money is not a problem, but the boys like chips and burgers best.

4 A couple looking for a snack after an evening's visit to the cinema. They would quite like to have an alcoholic drink with their meal.

5 A group of teenagers wanting a meal out together which is cheap but a little different.

To help you, here is an example of a report for the first group.

> If you are travelling in the South East and Midlands, then the McDonald's chain is a possible choice. The food is cheaper than in many other fast-food places, the service is very quick, except at peak times, and children are made to feel welcome. High chairs, toddler seats and badges are specially provided for them. Unfortunately there is no non-smoking area.
>
> Prices at the Happy Eater are higher, but there are branches throughout England and non-smoking areas have been set aside. The restaurants offer good food and service and are certainly geared to the needs of children, offering special menus, high chairs and even play areas at some branches. If you are prepared to pay a little more, this chain is better suited to your needs than the McDonald's chain.

Eating in your nearest town

Write a report about your local café or restaurant. Consider these factors:

Price
Opening times
Quality of service
Atmosphere
Quality and presentation of food
Standard of décor

CHOOSING A HOLIDAY

Here is a report on Kos, a Greek island, undertaken by *Which?*, a non-profit-making consumer magazine, followed by an advertisement for Kos in a holiday brochure.

A *Which?* report on Kos

Kos gets more touristy every year. But for the moment there's still something for everyone – a lively, interesting town; relaxed seaside villages, big isolated beach hotels, and excellent beaches. All the island lacks is charm. Mainly flat, agricultural and featureless. A single barren mountainous ridge in the south-east.

The busy and lively town and port of **Kos** is too developed to be architecturally or atmospherically charming, but is redeemed by luxuriant vegetation. Palms, mosques and Islamic-style architecture, a wide boulevard promenade with modern blocks. Long sandy beach north of harbour with watersports.

A popular alternative place to stay is **Kardamena** – friendly and relaxed, with lots of British, and miles of sandy beach. **Mastichari** is a quieter fishing village with a good beach.

Many interesting **things to see** in Kos town: antique sites, museum, fortress, sickly plane tree under which Hippocrates taught. Beautifully situated Hellenistic shrine behind Kos. Several old fortresses and monasteries. Numerous excursions – boats to nearby islands and Turkey, round the island bus tours, Greek evening.

Extensive **accommodation** in hotels and rooms in Kos; beach hotels around coast, some isolated. Rooms and small hotels in Kardamena, Mastichari, Tigaki.

Lots of sandy **beaches** near main places to stay – quieter ones elsewhere. Beautiful bay at Kamari (west).

Getting around: Fairly frequent buses from Kos to Kardamena, fewer to other villages. Cars, jeeps, mopeds and bicycles for hire in Kos. Boats Kos to Kamari.

Verdict   Good for: lively time, things to see, good beaches, tourist amenities. **Bad for:** pretty scenery, picturesque villages.

A holiday brochure on Kos

Kos is one of the most beautiful and picturesque islands in Greece and is fast becoming a very popular holiday island. Long and narrow, it is the second largest of the Dodecanese Islands, lying very close to the coast of Turkey. Birthplace of Hippocrates the 'father' of medicine, the island has been occupied by Romans, Turks and Italians, and has experienced both hard and happy times; but now it offers a friendly, informal holiday atmosphere. Green and fertile with an abundance of fresh water springs - it is sometimes called 'the garden of the Aegean Sea' - Kos is blessed with a delightful climate, wooded hillsides and green plains; numerous lovely beaches, calm seas and shallow waters, and a care-free lazy atmosphere which makes it ideal for a family holiday.

Kos Town
Kos Town is lively and welcoming; it is an attractive old township on the north-eastern shore of the island, with squares and streets lined with trees and flowers. The town and picturesque harbour are overlooked by the Castle of the Knights and there are numerous little bars, shops, discos and two beaches where there are good facilities for watersports.
Transfer time from Airport:
Approximately 45 minutes

Leisure/sightseeing
There is no shortage of interesting sites to be visited on Kos. The impressive Castle of the Knights of St.John is a fine building with many ancient sculptured statues; the massive Plane Tree said to have been planted by Hippocrates (legend has it that this was the spot where he taught). Near the Plane Tree is the Minaret of the elegant Turkish Mosque. In the central square in the middle of town is the Museum which houses an interesting collection of statues. By the harbour there is a part of the ancient town and the Temple of Dionyssos. Take a stroll through the Turkish Town and the colourful market place. Watersport facilities on the island are good and there is a popular sandy beach at Kardamena on the south coast. As the island is relatively flat, you can do your exploring by bike which is the most popular local transport. Excursions can be made to nearby islands, including the tiny islands of Kalymnos renowned for its sponge fishing, and Patmos with the Monastery of St.John and the Cave of the Apocalypse. A variety of evening entertainment is available on Kos, including nightclubs, discos, plenty of fish restaurants and folk dancing.

Shopping
Traditional embroidery, rugs and pullovers, pottery and olive-wood items make good gifts and souvenirs; bargains can also be found in furs and glassware.

Choice of words 1

Which? is not interested in selling a holiday, whereas a tour operator certainly is. This difference of purpose is reflected in the language. Make two columns. In the first, write words or phrases from the *Which?* report. In the second, write words or phrases from the brochure which either give a different and more attractive slant, or contradict the information in the *Which?* report. The first is done for you.

Which? report	Holiday brochure
Kos gets more touristy every year	Kos is fast becoming a very popular holiday island

Choice of words 2

Here are two entries about Kos from two more brochures. Make a list of words which have been chosen to make Kos sound attractive and which are also matters of *opinion* rather than fact. Which part of speech occurs in your list most frequently?

A beautiful Dodecanese island, near Rhodes, remains almost unspoilt, and unsophisticated, with some of the finest beaches in Greece. Hippocrates, the father of medicine, was born here and the pleasant climate, deep blue sea, Greek cuisine, bars and discos are just some of the healing properties this island possesses. The ancient town of Kos with its bougainvillea-covered houses and tree lined streets, leading down to the picturesque harbour provide a pleasant mixture of the old and new. Kos remains a good place for the unsophisticated pleasures and a delightful place to spend a relaxing holiday at a very interesting island.

Boat trips to the nearby island and excursions/tours within the island.

Kos, green and fertile, with citrus groves, mountainous ridges and marvellous near-deserted beaches, is an island of great charm. Dolphin-shaped and serene, lying only a few miles from the Turkish coast, it could almost be a miniature version of Rhodes. It has much the same history too – the Knights of St John built an impressive castle here and where once Turks and Venetians ruled, now holidaymakers laze away their days under a dependable blue sky and the hot Aegean sun.

The beaches fringing the island's coast are excellent and even in the height of summer you can find stretches of crowd-free, golden sand and hidden coves, tucked well away from the main trails. Tiny, whitewashed villages almost hidden under cascades of bright purple bougainvillea nestle beside calm, clear waters – at Kardamena, the village practically stands in the sea.

Kos Town is the island's capital, its lovely harbour guarded by a mediaeval castle. In the centre of the old town is Platanon Square where, under a spreading, gnarled old plane tree Kos' most famous son, Hippocrates, is said to have founded the world's first School of Medicine. Although the legend may seem unlikely, it's a lovely spot to sit and contemplate the delights of a holiday on Kos.

Write the advertisement that you imagine might have attracted this girl to go on this holiday.

Sifting the facts

Using the three brochure entries, make a list of all the *facts* given about Kos. Write a report on the island using all your facts.

Your favourite holiday spot

1 Write a report giving a factual account of a place you have visited on holiday. The purpose of the report is to guide future holidaymakers to make the right choice.
2 Write an entry in a holiday brochure for the same place. Your purpose is to attract people to buy your holiday, by presenting the place in the best possible light.

Making a choice

LANGUAGE PRACTICE

The language of newspapers

Read these two articles.

1

If the weather's bad . . .

BLAME THE COMPUTER IN FUTURE

That big black cloud forever hanging over the heads of Britain's weathermen has vanished.

Those 'Yah, ha-ha-got-it-wrong-again' remarks from the weather-conscious public won't trouble them too much any more.

For should that 'continuing dry' forecast develop into a depressing downpour they can blame the new member of the staff: Mr Comet.

Mr Comet – a £500,000 computer – joined the ranks of the Meteorological Office, Bracknell, Berkshire, yesterday.

He can scan half a million weather reports from all over the world – and come up with the answers in one and a half hours: blow, blaze, or below freezing.

He requires an operating staff of three and another 50 processors to feed in weather statistics. But he can cope with 1 million calculations a second. And he is hardly ever wrong.

Much faster

The introduction from today of regular computerised charts for weather forecasters was welcomed by the Meteorological Office's new director-general, 42-year-old Dr John Mason, who took over a month ago.

He described Mr Comet as 'a great stride forward'. For he admitted that the humble, human weatherman poring over his charts and figures can 'sometimes be wrong'.

Whereas Mr Comet, flashing and clicking away in his sunshine room at the top of the Meteorological Office, does the job just as well 'if not better' and almost five times as quickly.

Up to now Mr Comet's generalised weather charts have been compared each day with charts produced by the seven-to-ten-hour human process. The results are almost identical.

In a few more months Mr Comet will be such a trusted member of the staff that his charts will be accepted without a qualm. The forecasters will use them as the basis for the detailed bulletins.

Said Dr Mason: 'It will relieve the staff of a lot of donkey work.'

Already the Meteorological Office is thinking of a big brother for Mr Comet, who has a memory bank of a mere 50,000 words.

A bigger computer would cope with a hoped-for expansion in the number of world-wide weather stations and a bigger communications centre to handle more and faster-arriving information.

One of the Bracknell experts glanced at Mr Comet's current prediction of the weather to come. By the side of the computered chart was another produced by human hands.

He said: 'They both say the same thing, I'm afraid – cold winds and the first real frost of the winter.'

2

Weather Forecasting by Numbers

From Our Science Correspondent

Revolutions can begin quietly. One began yesterday at the Meteorological Office headquarters at Bracknell. For the first time in routine procedure an electronic computer contributed to the forecast chart published today on this page. To look at there is nothing special about the chart. The change for the forecaster was only that an extra aid was given him. As well as preparing his own forecast chart of pressure distribution – always the first step in forecasting – he received a second chart drawn from the computer-made calculations. For the issued chart he could make use of either or both as he pleased.

The Computer's Job

The job of the computer, known as 'Comet', has been made as nearly automatic as possible. Its first task is to select data. Every day there pour into Bracknell a little under half a million five-figure numbers – all meteorological information in code. It is quicker to give the lot to the computer than to attempt to arrange the data by hand. The computer is programmed to pick out all stations that make observations of wind and temperature at high levels, to take all observations from ships at sea, to reject observations of visibility, cloud and so on which do not concern it, and, for the rest, to select.

The next stage is one of analysis. From the information at its disposal the computer arrives, by interpolation, at values of sea-level pressure, or of heights of pressure surfaces, at an even network of grid points. It applies checks of consistency – but a few cases, such as the retention or rejection of a vital isolated report, are reserved to human judgment. All is now ready for the numerical forecast. This is carried forward step by step, looking only an hour ahead, or less, in any one step. This is being continued at present for 48 hours.

How will forecasts be affected? No dramatic change should be looked for. Too many needs have first to be met, each reacting on the others. One is for more information about high-level conditions above the Atlantic as a whole, the tropics, and surprisingly (from a British standpoint) the southern hemisphere. A second need is for research. Air, for example, is not a uniform fluid, but differs from place to place, and from time to time, in humidity. The relevant facts need to be included in the basic computation – not merely injected at the end, as an aid to 'putting weather into the forecast'. More, too, needs to be known about the working of the atmosphere as a whole. A third need is for more or bigger computers – not only to handle the increased amount of information but for research to enable information to be better used. Weather forecasting, so long an art based on science, is in process of becoming a branch of applied mathematics.

The differences

These two reports have the same content but different purposes.

1 **The presentation**

Study the differences between the two reports in terms of:

content of headlines
size of print
length of paragraphs
length of sentences
use and positioning of conjunctions
use of formal or informal language
choice of vocabulary
attitude towards the computer
tone

2 **A sense of drama**

The first report wishes to make the story lively and exciting. Among other devices, it uses colloquial language, and alliteration, and it takes the reader into its confidence. Find two examples of each of these devices.

3 **The story**

The reports take different angles on the same story. What are their angles? Find five short quotations from each report to illustrate the angle chosen.

4 **The purpose**

On the basis of what you have discovered so far, decide the purpose which each report has.

The similarities

Although the reports have contrasting purposes, they nevertheless share certain uses of language which are typical of newspaper style.

1 **Speech marks**

Find the nine examples of speech marks and say in each case why they have been used. Which uses are typical of newspapers?

2 **Word order**

Newspapers often use different word order for effect or emphasis.

FOR EXAMPLE:

> Said Dr Mason: 'It will relieve the staff of a lot of donkey work.'
> He said: 'They both say the same thing, I'm afraid – cold winds and the first real frost of the winter.'

Find more examples where you could change the word order. What is the difference in effect when you do so?

3 **Parenthesis**

Slipping extra pieces of information into a sentence by using asides or parentheses is an economical way of including some more information. For example:

> The job of the computer, known as 'Comet', has been made as nearly automatic as possible.

The parenthesis is marked off by commas.
Compare a similar sentence from the other article:

> Mr Comet – a £500,000 computer – joined the ranks of the Meteorological Office, Bracknell, Berkshire, yesterday.

What is the difference in the way these two sentences refer to the computer and its name?
Re-write one of these examples as two sentences. What is the difference now?
Find more examples from the passages, and re-write them in this way. Decide what the difference is.

4 **Dash**

Find three examples where a single dash is used. In each case replace the dash with a comma and decide what the difference is.

Can you identify?

These sentences are from sections of the articles which were omitted. Can you tell which article each is from? Give as many reasons as you can for your choice.

> Forecast pressure on contour heights at the chosen grid points can be printed out automatically at any stage.

> For Dr Mason said yesterday that his human staff had 'just about' reached the limit where their minds just couldn't absorb any more information.

Your own newspaper report

Here is an outline of a story. Write it up as a newspaper report in the style of the first article. Remember to include quotations from the people concerned.

An owl has nested in a housing estate in Hull. It is overprotective towards its two babies.

It has attacked at least seven people. Gary Knight, aged 22, was cut in the back of the neck. Another victim was knocked over and cut in the cheek. A man was attacked in broad daylight while mending his car.

The nest is in a tree near an old people's home.

The local RSPCA inspector has advised people to keep away from the area.

AUSTRIA

ALPBACH

Recommended

Excellent

Not extensive

Resort Altitude:
1000m/3281ft
Highest Lift Altitude:
1860m/6102ft

THE SKIER Alpbach is especially good for beginners. The nursery slopes are close to the village and have their own baby lifts, and the ski school is particularly well organised, with a high percentage of the instructors speaking English. After the first few days, beginners are then taken to the Wiedersbergerhorn area – the very efficient minibus service takes 4 minutes – and the two-stage chair lifts to further nursery slopes just below the Hornboden restaurant. Alpbach is also an excellent resort for intermediates. The main skiing access is via the Wiedersbergerhorn chairlifts – the shuttle bus service is free to lift pass holders. From the top station there are two drag lifts. The Mülden lift gives access to easy-medium runs, and the Brandegg to more advanced ones. Further access to the skiing is from Inneralpbach, reached in 6 minutes by shuttle-bus. The Galtenberg drag-lift and the Pögl chairlift lead to the Wiedersbergerhorn and more difficult runs over mainly northfacing slopes. There is a long semi off-piste run here, which is well within the reach of the intermediate skier.

THE NON SKIER
There is a large indoor pool with sauna, massage, solarium and glorious mountain views. At tea-time the Jakoberwirt serves a delicious variety of cakes and the Alphof serves terrific ice cream sundaes. There are shops, including one at the Gasthof Post which sells traditional 'dirndls'. Excursions can be arranged to Innsbruck, the Rattenberg glass factories, and further afield to Salzburg or Sterzing in Italy.

CHILDREN
There is a very good kindergarten taking children over 3, and the over 5's can join Ski Kindergarten. Evening babysitting can be arranged through the Tourist Office.

APRÈS SKI
Alpbach is a lively and informal place at night, with plenty of choice. Evenings often start with a drink at the Jakoberwirt – centrally situated on the village square, this old inn has lots of atmosphere and a bar serving good draught beer. The Postillian pub, below the Post Hotel, is popular with locals and guests alike. Much of the entertainment organised by the representative takes place at the Hotel Alphof – fondue parties, Tyrolean evenings and raclette parties are all followed by music and dancing. Another popular evening is the sleigh ride to the Rossmoos, where after losing your inhibitions over a few schnapps you can learn to yodel and try schühplatter dancing! The week always ends with the traditional ski school prize giving, where even if you've not won anything you can have a final dance and drink with your fellow classmates and ski teacher.

▭▭▭▣▷ *EXAMINATION PRACTICE*

Directed writing 1

Imagine you have arranged with a friend (or group of friends) to go on your first skiing holiday. You have to make the final choice of resort from the three advertised on page 178 and below.

Read the advertisements carefully, trying to separate fact from opinion and travel agents' exaggeration.

Make brief notes from each of the three advertisements, decide which is the best for your purposes and in about 150 words give the reasons for your choice.

AUSTRIA
SEEFELD

Excellent   Good   Not recommended

Resort Altitude:
1180m/3872ft
Highest Lift Altitude:
2100m/6890ft

THE SKIER Seefeld is ideally suited to beginners who can try their first tentative runs on the gentle nursery slopes of the Geigenbuhel, just over ten minutes' walk from the village centre – and very close to the Enterprise hotels. Seefeld's excellent ski school has over 150 instructors, many of them English-speaking. A free bus service links the two skiing areas – The Gschwandtkopf area is on the south-west side of the village, with two parallel chair lifts rising from the bottom station. One terminates half-way up, the other rises to the top where there is a restaurant. There is a drag to the left of this system, plus a chair lift from Reith, and all the runs are easy and ideal for 1st and 2nd year skiers. Intermediates will prefer the Rosshütte area, on the north-eastern side of the village. Its alternately open and wooded slopes offer exciting challenges to better skiers, especially in the descents from Seefelderjoch (6780ft) and Harmelekopf (6890ft). Alternatively you can ski on the open sunny slopes around the restaurant where there are two drag lifts. The runs from Rosshütte, which follow the line of the mountain railway back to the upper limits of the village, are not too difficult – in all, Seefeld's 16 miles of varied ski runs take in eight marked pistes. Seefeld is also superb for the cross-country skier, with 100 miles of tracks plus specialised tuition.
THE NON-SKIER
Seefeld offers possibly the widest range of non-ski activities of any wintersports resort. Ski bobbing, tobogganing, curling, ice-skating and ski jumping are available. Swimmers can choose from a multitude of heated pools. There are also saunas, indoor tennis courts, a bowling alley, horse-riding facilities, and over 60 kms of cleared paths where you can wander through magnificent countryside. Seefeld itself is delightful for sightseeing and its cafés and bars are temptingly numerous. The nearby city of Innsbruck is well worth a visit and excursions can also be made to Salzburg, Oberammergau in W. Germany and Sterzing in Italy.
CHILDREN
A separate ski school caters for children from 6 years upwards and a ski kindergarten for the 4-6's. Supervised lunches are also available.
APRÈS SKI
Night-life is abundant in Seefeld and caters for every taste and pocket. Early starters can catch the late afternoon dances in the centrally situated Café Corso and the Tenne. Later on choose from a wide variety of cinemas, restaurants, night clubs and discos. Many hotels hold fondue evenings and traditional bars áre marvellous for a rowdy Tyrolean get together. More formal – a jacket and tie is required – is the casino, where gamblers can enjoy a spree at Baccarat, Chemin de Fer or roulette.

AUSTRIA
ZELL AM ZILLER

Good   Excellent   Good Ziller Valley choices

Resort Altitude:
580m/1902ft
Highest Lift Altitude:
2264m/7428ft

THE SKIER Zell am Ziller's runs are very well suited to the beginner, who is advised to purchase a lift pass locally in order to best suit his/her needs. *All* skiers need a lift pass. The Ski School meets at the Rosenalm nursery slopes and there are several easy runs in this area. The intermediate is also well served – The Kreuzjoch gondola takes skiers to Gründelalm (3,356ft) where the skiing commences (there is no skiing back to the village from this side). From Gründelalm a chair lift rises to Rosenalm (5,774ft). It is a large, sunny bowl, served by 3 drag lifts. 3 further drags serve the Enzianhof area and to ski back to Gründelalm an intermediate run follows the chair lift. The Gerlosstein area is a little over 3 miles from Zell am Ziller, and over 1,000ft higher. A frequent bus service (free to skiers) takes one to the bottom stage of the cable car (3,306ft) in 13 minutes. The top station is at 5,142ft and there are two drags and a chair lift, the Arbiskogel, which rises to 6,019ft. Runs back to the middle station are intermediate and there is also a good one to the bottom station – it is often used for races but snow conditions can close it later in the season. For better skiers, Zell am Ziller's position makes it ideal as a base for skiing all the resorts covered by the Ziller Superpass. People with this pass are allowed to travel free on the trains up and down the valley – provided they are skiing – but a car has a distinct advantage too. It should be pointed out that this pass covers the lifts at Hintertux, where there is glacier skiing throughout the year. This is a real boon in years when local conditions are less than perfect!
THE NON SKIER
A non-skiers' pass is available, giving access (afternoons only on certain lifts) to lots of mountain sunshine and glorious scenery – and pleasant restaurants with large sun terraces. Early in the season, whilst snow conditions allow, there is tobogganing and skating and an indoor tennis court. Coach excursions can be booked to Innsbruck, Salzburg and Hintertux. The village itself is well worth exploring, with a beautiful 18th century church, and not too far away a very interesting folk museum, the Wurzensepp. You may also be able to arrange a visit to the Zillertal Brewery – the oldest one in the Tyrol.
APRÈS SKI Zell am Ziller offers all the traditional night-time entertainment you would expect from an Austrian resort – schuhplatter evenings, barbecues, Tyrolean evenings and of course numerous discos or live music if you prefer. One of the most popular nightspots is the Dorfstadl, where you can enjoy a Tyrolean evening or the Austrian "Party Night". Or try your hand at nine-pin bowling. Every Friday evening the ski school prize-giving takes place – a must to round off your holiday.

Making a choice

Directed writing 2

Imagine you are employed either by the British Tourist Board or a local tourist area. You have been asked to design an advertisement to counter the increasing success of foreign countries in attracting British tourists.

Make a list of what either Britain as a whole or the particular area of your choice has to offer holiday-makers. Choose what you think are the most important points on your list and design your advertisement. (You can, if you wish, stress some negative points about foreign travel, such as extra cost, delays at airports, customs, uncertainties of exchange rates.)

11 Your point of view

*This section helps you to discover, test and organise your views on one topic –
the image created by what a person wears. The method can be followed for
other topics, some of which are suggested at the end of the section.*

You are asked to

⟶ **Complete a questionnaire**

⟶ **Analyse and interpret the results of a survey**

⟶ **Give advice based on the survey**

⟶ **Take a role in a discussion**

⟶ **Draw conclusions from a transcript of a discussion**

⟶ **Examine the different uses of direct and reported speech**

⟶ **Write a report**

⟶ **Write an article expressing your views**

⟶ **Criticise students' work on the same subject**

⟶ **Respond to a series of views without preparation**

Examination practice – study arguments given on a topic and discuss the points raised

YOUR IMAGE AT WORK

How important are the clothes people wear at work?

Copy out and complete this questionnaire. It was designed by *Which?* magazine to reveal what people think about the clothes they choose for work.

Tick the appropriate box	Agree	Disagree	Neither
The way people dress at work usually shows how competent they are at their job.			
People should be allowed to wear exactly what they want to at work.			
Firms who want employees to wear particular clothes should pay for these clothes.			
People who wear inappropriate clothes are likely to be unsuitable for responsible positions.			
In most firms the way you dress will affect your chances of promotion.			
People work best in clothes they feel most comfortable in.			
People who wear unusual clothes to work are generally more imaginative.			
People wearing unusual clothes to work give a bad impression to clients.			
As long as people are good at their job it shouldn't matter what they wear.			
It is old fashioned to expect people to wear certain clothes for work.			
I object to senior female staff wearing trousers.			
I object to junior female staff wearing trousers.			
Sloppy clothes mean sloppy work.			
I wouldn't have faith in an executive who wore jeans to work.			
Men shouldn't be allowed to take off their jackets at work even in the summer.			
Bosses should always be smartly dressed.			

Class work

Collect the results for your class by counting the number of ticks in each box for each statement. Write down the numbers on your own questionnaire so that you each have a record of the survey.
Where were you most in agreement?
Where were you least in agreement?

Compare the results of your survey with these results from the *Which?* survey based on a sample of over a thousand people.

What differences are there between your results and the *Which?* results?

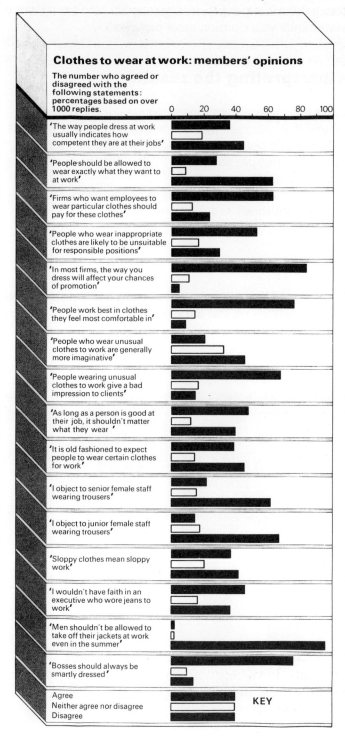

Clothes to wear at work: members' opinions

The number who agreed or disagreed with the following statements: percentages based on over 1000 replies.

'The way people dress at work usually indicates how competent they are at their jobs'

'People should be allowed to wear exactly what they want to at work'

'Firms who want employees to wear particular clothes should pay for these clothes'

'People who wear inappropriate clothes are likely to be unsuitable for responsible positions'

'In most firms, the way you dress will affect your chances of promotion'

'People work best in clothes they feel most comfortable in'

'People who wear unusual clothes to work are generally more imaginative'

'People wearing unusual clothes to work give a bad impression to clients'

'As long as a person is good at their job, it shouldn't matter what they wear'

'It is old fashioned to expect people to wear certain clothes for work'

'I object to senior female staff wearing trousers'

'I object to junior female staff wearing trousers'

'Sloppy clothes mean sloppy work'

'I wouldn't have faith in an executive who wore jeans to work'

'Men shouldn't be allowed to take off their jackets at work even in the summer'

'Bosses should always be smartly dressed'

KEY
Agree
Neither agree nor disagree
Disagree

183

Analysing the results

1 Which four statements did most people agree with?
2 Which four statements did most people disagree with?
3 Over which four statements was opinion most divided?

Discussion – interpreting the results

Why do you think some people object to women wearing trousers?
What evidence is there that attitudes to jeans might be changing?
Most agree that people work best in the clothes they find comfortable, yet a majority did not agree that people should be allowed to wear what they want at work. Can you explain this contradiction?
What evidence is there in the results that people consider smart dress to be important for someone ambitious?

Summary

Write a paragraph giving advice to someone starting a new job and keen to be successful. Base your advice on this survey.

Specialised clothing
What work do you think these people are going to do? Write 200–250 words.

YOUR IMAGE AT SCHOOL

Role-play

A group of students of your own age held a discussion in the form of a role-play about the importance of school uniform. Here is the information they were given about a particular school and its uniform.

The situation

The school

Spurley School is situated on the edge of a large town. Its catchment area includes a mixture of Victorian terraced housing, a council estate, a modern private housing estate, and some large town houses. The school is a large, mixed comprehensive – 1,500 pupils – and has a good reputation, particularly for examination results.

Uniform in the school

The uniform has been the same since the school opened. Pupils wear a maroon blazer, maroon jumper, maroon and grey tie, white shirt, grey skirt for girls and black trousers for boys.

   Now there is a feeling emerging from some parents, children and staff that the uniform needs up-dating; some even feel that there is no need at all for a uniform. The Head has called a small committee of people to have an initial discussion.

The roles

1 *Head* believes that:
   — a smart uniform creates a good impression both in school and outside.
   — a uniform makes the gap between pupils from rich and poor backgrounds less obvious.
   — high standards of uniform mean high standards of work and discipline.
   — the present uniform is perhaps rather dull and dowdy.
   — if the uniform were changed, standards might slip because pupils might take advantage during the changeover.

2 *Parent with one child at the school* believes that:
   — smart uniform creates a good impression.
   — the present uniform is too expensive.
   — a replacement uniform would simply add to the expense.
   — the present uniform is dull.
   — a change would be good if it did not involve any extra expense.

3 *Teacher* believes that:
- uniform at present is often scruffy.
- uniform is difficult to enforce because many pupils hate it.
- uniform will need to be changed every five years to stay up to date.
- it does not affect standards of behaviour and work, but it does create a good impression on visitors and on the community.

4 *Student* believes that:
- uniform does not influence behaviour or work.
- you can still tell who comes from a rich and who from a poor family.
- most pupils hate uniform.
- pupils grow out of the blazer quickly and it is expensive to replace.

5 *Student* believes that:
- having a uniform means that leisure clothes stay smart for longer.
- you would waste time every morning if you had to worry about what you had to wear.
- pupils would be trying to impress each other with their clothes.
- it is more relaxing to come home and change out of your uniform.

6 *Representative from the shop which supplies the uniforms* believes that:
- the present uniform is as cheap as any uniform can be.
- the blazer is the most expensive item. Can this be replaced by another item of clothing?
- if the design of the skirt were relaxed, this might give parents more scope for choosing cheaper ones.
- it is not perhaps necessary for the girls to wear a tie. They could then wear blouses.
- the shop is interested in any changes made in uniform but is very concerned that if the school abandons uniform it will lose business.

Chairperson and secretary

Two pupils in the group performed these two jobs as well as their own role.

Job of chairperson
- open the meeting and introduce the representatives.
- outline the topic to be discussed.
- start the discussion by asking one person to give his/her views.
- guide the discussion by preventing arguments, allowing everyone to have a say and moving into another area if the discussion reaches a stalemate.
- keep people to the subject.

Job of secretary

— keep notes of the points people make.
— ask if you feel there is something you haven't understood or followed.
— after the meeting write up the notes so that they are logical and easy to follow.

Transcript of the role-play

The group divided the roles among them. Caroline played the headmistress and also chairperson, Louise the shop representative and secretary, Roy a teacher, Sarah a pupil and Paul a parent. Here is a transcript of part of their discussion.

Caroline (Head)	Well . . . um . . . as you know the uniform is of a maroon colour with a maroon tie and er I have heard that the pupils would like this changed and I . . . er . . . don't know whether I agree or not but I suppose it should be changed since it is quite expensive. Now Miss Rogers, how much does the average blazer cost?	1 5
Louise (Shop rep.)	Around £32.	
Caroline (Chairperson)	£32?	
Louise	Yes.	
Caroline	As you can see, that is very expensive and the pupils have suggested to me a sweatshirt in replacement of . . . a blazer. This should be passed to the pupils to see what their view is. Sarah would you like to put your views on sweat-shirts?	10
Sarah	Oh um . . . well um . . . I think the whole sort of uniform is stupid really because it doesn't influence our work or behaviour or anything. I . . .	15
Caroline	What do you mean by that?	
Sarah	I mean the whole sort of point of the uniform is to be smart and that but . . . um . . . otherwise there's not much point.	20
Caroline	But do you agree that a uniform makes you look smart?	
Sarah	Depends what sort of uniform.	
Caroline	Well, our uniform. Don't you think it makes you pupils look smart?	
Sarah	It would have done ten years ago but . . . styles . . .	25
Roy	The uniform we've got at the moment – often it's very	

scruffy though with . . . cos er pupils don't like it. But if we changed it more often pupils would look smarter.

Caroline Yes, but there's a great expense in changing the uniform so often. How often would . . .   30

Roy Well ev . . .

Sarah Yes but if you . . .

Caroline Can I interrupt you, Sarah? Let Mr Cusworth finish.

Roy Every five years.

Caroline Yes but then parents might have to buy two lots of uniform.   35

Sarah Excuse me, can I say something please?

Caroline Yes, carry on.

Sarah I think if pupils dislike the uniform they're wearing at the moment they could wear it in a smarter way with sweat-shirts for boys and girls.   40

Roy I think that would look scruffy.

Caroline Why do you think it would look scruffy?

Roy Well, blazers look smart and . . .

Caroline We seem to be reaching the point where we all think something needs to be changed. I'd like to hear every-one's opinion on sweatshirts or blazers.   45

The students

These pupils reveal much about themselves in the role-play.

1 Who is the dominant person in the group?
2 Who is the shyest?
3 At what points in this discussion does Caroline show herself to be a good chairperson?
4 Who has learnt how to use the chairperson to add to the discussion?

The secretary's job

Louise's job was to make notes so that she could write a report afterwards, in which she outlined the main points of discussion.

Reported speech

Compare these two versions. The first is what was actually said. This is called *direct speech*. The second is Louise's report. It is written in *reported speech*.

Read them and then make a list of the *differences* between them. Look particularly at the verbs.

1 **Caroline** Now Miss Rogers, how much does the average blazer cost?
  Louise Around £32.
  Caroline £32?
  Louise Yes.
  Caroline As you can see, that is very expensive . . .

2 Miss Rogers told the meeting that an average blazer cost £32. The headmistress thought that was very expensive.

Turn the following piece of direct speech into reported speech.

Caroline But do you agree that a uniform makes you look smart?
  Sarah Depends what sort of uniform.
Caroline Well, our uniform. Don't you think it makes you pupils look smart?
  Sarah It would have done ten years ago . . .

Writing the report

Make notes from the transcript of the main points and write them up as a report.

Your own role-play

In groups of six, each choose one of the roles outlined and prepare for a discussion on school uniform. The notes on the roles are only intended as guidelines to help you start your discussion. Add your own notes until you feel confident about the point of view you are representing. Two people will need to volunteer as chairperson and secretary as well. It is the chairperson's function to make sure that some kind of decision is reached by the end of the meeting.

Writing a report

Each member of the group should take a copy of the secretary's notes and write a report of the meeting. Compare reports. Whose was the best? Why?

Reporting to the class

One member of each group should report its conclusions to the whole class. Did each group have different thoughts on the question of school uniform? Did any group produce a completely new uniform?

WRITING ABOUT A POINT OF VIEW

Preparation in pairs

Imagine that you have been asked to produce an article, about 200 words long, on uniform, for your school magazine or newspaper. One of you is to put the case in favour of uniform, and the other against. Prepare for your essay.

1 Make a list together of all the arguments on both sides you can think of.

2 One person then states one of the arguments and the other challenges by questioning. Here is an example:

A: Uniform is too expensive.
B: What do you mean by too expensive? How much did you pay for your uniform? Is it more expensive than ordinary clothes? Is it expensive in the long term or just the short term?

In doing this, you will enable each other to *develop* your arguments rather than simply stating them briefly.

3 Organise your arguments into the best *structure* so that there is some connection and development of ideas.

4 Choose a title for your article.

ANOTHER POINT OF VIEW

Interpretation and comment

Opposite are extracts from an examination board's 1984 table of results for 'O' level and 'A' level.

The records for 'O' level show the number of entries and the percentage passing at Grade 'C' (the middle grade) or above.

The records for 'A' level show the number of entries and the percentage passing at high grades, A or B.

Study the tables and write a 450–500 word response to them. Your response should deal with three factors:

a) What the patterns of entries and successes for boys and girls show.
b) Your interpretation of the results – why there are such differences in entries and successes for boys and girls, for example.
c) Your views on whether attempts should be made to alter the pattern. Either make suggestions for encouraging a different pattern of entry or give reasons why you think the present pattern is satisfactory.

	Boys	**16+ Examination**	Girls	
Subject	Entries	% passing at Grade 'C' or above	Entries	% passing at Grade 'C' or above
English Language	18922	62.8	25735	62.6
English Literature	11385	53.0	18211	60.5
Woodwork	1811	62.0	36	61.1
Music	993	55.0	2616	63.1
Physics	7873	61.7	4566	62.3
Home Economics	52	65.4	1181	75.0
Maths	5887	66.7	6518	60.9
French	3797	60.7	7929	66.7
Political Studies	1130	59.0	914	52.4

	Boys	**Advanced Level**	Girls	
Subject	Entries	% awarded grades A or B	Entries	% awarded grades A or B
English Literature	1698	20.5	5250	24.4
Physics	2693	28.2	953	27.2
Maths	2957	32.4	1517	31.6
French	632	26.3	2299	25.1
Engineering	92	26.1	Nil	
Home Economics (Dress and Fabrics)	1	100.0	207	30.4
Computer Science	421	27.8	75	20.0

▭▭▭▷ *LANGUAGE PRACTICE*

Giving a talk – your opinion

Here are seven topics for discussion.

1 Should the retirement age be lowered to fifty?
2 Have the campaigners for animal rights the right themselves to vandalise research laboratories and endanger people's lives?
3 Should people who have chosen to make themselves ill by smoking be treated by the National Health Service?
4 Are co-educational schools better for both sexes than single-sex schools?
5 Is trial by jury the fairest way of obtaining justice?
6 Since we are members of the Common Market, should we change to driving on the right-hand side of the road?
7 How much have computers affected our lives?

Preparing a talk

1 *In pairs* (A and B)
Choose one topic. A should take one side of the argument and B the other. Spend ten minutes listing your arguments on paper. Then hold your discussion. Try to find arguments in response to what your partner is saying.

2 *In pairs*
Choose another topic. Each partner spends ten minutes preparing both sides of the argument. Then each speaks for thirty seconds. Tape your speeches and judge them using these questions to help you:
Was the speech smooth and fluent or full of hesitations?
Did the speaker stick to the subject?
Did the speaker manage to find three or four convincing arguments?
Was the speaker able to see both sides of the question?

3 *Solo, in front of the class*
Choose a topic, either a new one or one you have already prepared. Prepare a two minute talk on the subject like this:

a) Write down everything you wish to say. Read it through and check that your arguments are in the right order, that each point connects with the one before and that you have chosen interesting examples to illustrate your point of view.
b) On a separate piece of paper, write down a key word or phrase which sums up each stage of your talk.
c) Give your talk to the rest of the class using only this piece of paper.

Before you prepare your talk read this draft of a talk with a teacher's comments in the margin. You will find a list of the key phrases from the talk on page 194.

Should people who have chosen to make themselves ill by smoking be treated by the National Health?

good idea to have a visual prop and to ask a question - seizes the audience's attention right away.

Here is a cigarette packet. On the side of it it says 'Cigarettes can seriously damage your health'. So anybody who smokes does it knowing exactly the harm that is involved. Should such a person then have the right to be paid for by the rest of us when he or she gets lung cancer or heart trouble or any of the other smoking-related diseases?

You've illustrated your point that everybody knows it's been proved.

Everybody knows it's now been totally proved that smoking damages your health. There have been programmes on television showing people dying in pain because of smoking. We've seen pictures of the healthy lungs of non-smokers and the diseased lungs of smokers. We get shown a film at school too, so if we start smoking we know what we are risking.

Examples from personal experience are a good idea. They make your talk more human and interesting.

My uncle smokes forty a day and has a bad cough, particularly in the morning. There is nothing wrong with him at the moment, but his doctor has warned him about bronchitis. My uncle knows the risks but he won't stop. He says it's his pleasure in life. But why should he make other people pay for his pleasure?

My dad was supposed to give up smoking some years ago for his health. But I know he goes out into the garden for a few crafty fags on the quiet. I sympathise with people who are addicted, but why should the rest of us pay for them?

Again you've given examples to support your point.

Society is now making more moves against smoking. It's completely banned from the London Underground. Many cafés have non-smoking areas set aside. So do aeroplanes and trains and cinemas. There is much more pressure on smokers now. More and more people are giving up smoking.

In the end it's the Government to blame. They need the tax from the cigarettes and so they won't take a firm stand on it. They should ban smokers from being treated by the National Health.

A good attempt to interest your audience and follow through an argument. But it's a little short at the moment. Perhaps you should redraft the last paragraph. It's rather abrupt and treated too briefly. Also, although you obviously feel strongly about the issue, you should present arguments from the opposite point of view. For example, it would be very difficult to ban smokers from National Health treatment, because smoking may be only one of many causes of a person's illness. You cannot always prove a direct connection between smoking and a disease.

Key phrases

1 Packet warning
2 Everybody knows smoking damages health and examples.
3 My uncle
4 My dad
5 Moves against smoking
6 Government – they should ban.

▭▭▷ *EXAMINATION PRACTICE*

Read this passage from *Genesis* by Brian Morris.

The last word

1 'Who are you?' said the Prime Minister, opening the door.
'I am God,' replied the stranger.
'I don't believe you,' sneered the Prime Minister. 'Show me a miracle.'
And God showed the Prime Minister the miracle of birth.
5 'Pah,' said the Prime Minister. 'My scientists are creating life in test-tubes
and have nearly solved the secret of heredity. Artificial insemination is more
certain than your lackadaisical method, and by cross-breeding we are
producing fish and mammals to our design. Show me a proper miracle.'
And God caused the sky to darken and hailstones came pouring down.
10 'That's nothing,' said the Prime Minister, picking up the telephone to the Air
Ministry. 'Send up a met. plane would you, old chap, and sprinkle the clouds
with silver chloride crystals.'
And the met. plane went up and sprinkled the clouds which had darkened
the world and the hailstones stopped pouring down and the sun shone
15 brightly.
'Show me another,' said the Prime Minister.
And God caused a plague of frogs to descend upon the land.
The Prime Minister picked up his telephone. 'Get the Min. of Ag. and Fish,'
he said to the operator, 'and instruct them to procure a frog-killer as
20 myxomatosis killed rabbits.'
And soon the land was free of frogs, and the people gave thanks to the
Prime Minister and erected laboratories in his name.
'Show me another,' sneered the Prime Minister.
And God caused the sea to divide.
25 The Prime Minister picked up his direct-link telephone to the Polaris
submarine. 'Lob a few ICBMs into Antarctica and melt the ice-cap, please, old
man.'

And the ice-cap melted into water and the sea came rushing back.
'I will kill all the first-born,' said God.
30 'Paltry tricks,' said the Prime Minister. 'Watch this.' He pressed a button on his desk. And missiles flew to their pre-ordained destination and H-bombs split the world asunder and radio-activity killed every mortal thing.
'I can raise the dead,' said God.
'Please,' said the Prime Minister in his cardboard coffin. 'Let me live again.'
35 'Why, who are you?' said God, closing the lid.

Genesis by Brian Morris

Answer in note form the following questions on issues raised by the passage. Then discuss your views in groups of 6–8. One member of each group should be chosen to report the group's feelings to the rest of the class.

1 In what ways has man's increasing ability to influence nature been beneficial?
2 In what ways has it been harmful?
3 Are nuclear weapons a necessary evil?
4 What limitation of man's power is illustrated by the passage? What other limitations are there?

A choice of school

Below are the basic facts about two schools. Study them and write two paragraphs of 10–15 lines:

1 setting out your reasons for choosing one of the schools.
2 outlining the further information you would like before committing yourself to your choice.

Maxwell Comprehensive (Mixed)

1,691 pupils aged 11–19, 197 in sixth form. Modern buildings, small playgrounds, 11 mobile classrooms. Pupils placed in sets based on ability from the first year. Good examination results. Rather limited choice of subjects.

Johnson High

487 girls aged 11–16 (transfer to Sixth Form College available). Old buildings with some recent modernisation. Playground and sports field space generous. Classes taught in mixed ability classes throughout. Wide choice of subject. Social development considered more important than examination results. *Note* Johnson High may be considered an all-boys' school for the purpose of the exercise.

12 A matter of tact

Letters, memos, leaflets

Letters are usually written to a particular person. This means you need to be more than usually careful to catch the right tone.

You are asked to

——————➤ Answer a letter of complaint

——————➤ Write tactful memos to colleagues

——————➤ Prepare an advertising leaflet

——————➤ Write a letter of complaint

——————➤ Arrange and take part in a conference

——————➤ Apply by letter for a job

——————➤ Complete an application form

——————➤ Apply by telephone for a job

——————➤ Hold an interview for a job

——————➤ Consider the use of appropriate language

Examination practice – write a letter or a report and a piece of prose

LETTERS – CATCHING THE RIGHT TONE

Write three tasks from instructions

You are employed by the Quicksure School of Motoring as the secretary to the owner, Mr Thomson. He is away for two days and has left you three jobs.

> 37, Cedar Rd.,
> Darton
>
> 3/10/86
>
> Dear Sir,
>   I have now had five driving lessons with your instructor, Mr Wallis. All five of them have been spent starting, stopping and turning on a little country road outside town. I suggested to Mr Wallis that I ought to be practising in town, especially as my uncle had been teaching me for six months before I joined your driving school.
>   But he wouldn't let me, and last Thursday when I asked for the third time if I could go into town he said: 'You're not yet fit to drive a bike with stabilisers if you want to know the truth.'
>   I'm not paying out seven pounds an hour to be insulted. I want a new instructor or I'll go somewhere else, and I want to start driving properly in town. I have to take my test next month, because I'm getting a new job that involves driving.
>   I just don't get on with Mr Wallis. He is such a miserable, moaning person who snaps at the slightest thing.
>   If Mr Wallis is there when I come for my lesson on Thursday, I'll turn round and go straight to the British School of Motoring.
>   Yours faithfully,
>   Ian Charlton.

Mr Thomson has left you a note:

> Ask Joe Wallis what's been going on and then write to Mr Charlton. Get Joe to apologise if he said what the chap claims. Let Maura Davidson take over — but do it without upsetting Joe too much. We don't want to lose him. He's a good instructor — wish he wouldn't be so prickly.
>
> Good Luck!

Below is the office memo used for internal communications. This means for sending messages within the office. Copy it out and send an enquiry to Joe Wallis. Choose what you tell him carefully. Remember your purpose is to keep Joe, the customer (and your boss) as happy as possible.

Quicksure School of Motoring	INTERNAL MEMO
Date:	
From:	To:
Subject Matter:	
Enquiry:	
Reply:	

Look at Joe's reply on the next page.

> Yes, I did say something of the sort – I also said I was sorry. He kept up a constant stream of moans, about not driving in town. Trouble is he's learnt all the wrong things from his uncle. For instance, at corners he depresses the clutch, free-wheels round and then changes gear. He's NOT SAFE in a town – he's hardly safe starting up. Amateur teaching is getting more of a problem – They're much better off coming to us without a clue.

Write – be tactful

a) A further note to Joe asking for a short letter of apology for you to send to Mr Charlton and telling him you are getting Maura Davidson to take over.
b) A note to Maura Davidson asking her to take Mr Charlton. She will need details. What warnings will you give her?
c) The letter to Mr Charlton. Do you warn him that he is unlikely to pass his test in a month? Do you mention his bad driving habits as an explanation? He will need to know about his new instructor.
   Joe has sent you a note. It says:

> Mr Charlton. I'm sorry about what I said. Joe Wallis.

Do you include it or just make some reference to Joe's apology?

Mr Thomson's second note:

> I'm trying to pep up business at the young end of the market – 6 lesson course for under 21s for £40 – maybe even lower if they book a course of 10 or 20. What do you think? I also want to offer a credit scheme – start learning now but pay over a year. Prepare a handbill for me to look at when I get back – give prominence to our 83 per cent first time pass rate – mention the instructional and safety videos they can see free at the office. Include usual details about expert, friendly instructors (perhaps we can get Joe to smile a bit more!)

Prepare the handbill. You will need practical details (when does the offer start, for instance) that are not in the notes.

Mr Thomson's third note:

> It's taking Warley Garage far too long to repair minor bumps and scratches on our cars. I saw Joe Wallis yesterday giving a lesson in a car with a buckled front bumper. He says he's contacted Warley – They say They can't do it for a fortnight. Major Danby has a similar tale, I think. We just can't afford to give lessons in battered cars – it's the worst possible image. Get details and write to Warley (the manager is Alan Geeson) – tell them if They can't do better we'll have to go elsewhere – we pay them for a better service than that.

Write the letter, having taken details from the two instructors. Make the position clear, without being rude.

Hold a conference

When Mr Thomson comes back he intends to hold a conference with all the driving instructors. The two main items on the agenda are:

1 Ways to increase business.
Mr Thomson will outline his proposal for cheaper rates for under 21s and ask for other suggestions.

2 The Association of Examiners is planning to petition the Government to make the driving test more efficient. The Association has invited all schools of motoring to comment on its proposals and suggest others. Mr Thomson wants his staff's views. The suggestions are

a) Varying routes more so that candidates cannot simply practise the few known routes the test takes.
b) Testing night and motorway driving.
c) A better eyesight test – perhaps a doctor's certificate.
d) A compulsory five-lesson course with a driving school.

Mr Thomson

Joe Wallis

Maura Davidson

Marjorie Andrews

Geraldine Shaw

Major Danby

Hold the conference in groups of six, each person taking the part of one of these people.

Charles Thomson
He will chair the conference. His main interest is in increasing business.

Joe Wallis – aged 58
Has been with the firm longer than the present owner. He is against change, especially gimmicks. He likes to work regular hours. He believes people take the test too soon. His general attitude is – 'If they take time to learn properly, they can drive anywhere at any time.'

Maura Davidson – aged 27
Young – two years with the firm but well-liked by pupils. She has definite ideas about increasing business, including working late at night to give people opportunities after they have finished work. Generally welcomes a stiffer driving test.

Marjorie Andrews – aged 60
Excellent with older pupils who are over-cautious and lacking confidence. Wants to make a feature of attracting them to Quicksure. Tends to reminisce about driving instruction when she first began. Does, however, think the present test outdated considering modern conditions.

Geraldine Shaw – is the secretary of the county's branch of the Driving Instructors' Association. Has been invited to the meeting at the instigation of Maura Davidson. Geraldine is particularly concerned about the long hours and general stress of a driving instructor's job. Would not like new practices without increased benefits for instructors.

Major Danby
Joined the firm after long service as an instructor in the army. Has always thought the driving test too easy, and has suggestions for improvements. Thinks that the best way of attracting customers is a near 100 per cent first-time pass rate. Would reject pupils after two lessons if they were likely failures.

Summary

After the conference each person should write a two paragraph report (in character) of what happened.

Applying for a job

In applying for jobs from the advertisements on the opposite page, you will need to take part in a certain amount of role-play. You can invent certain qualifications and experience, and may, if you wish, invent a new personality, as well as making yourself considerably older.

Writing 1

Choose one of the jobs where you are asked to apply in writing and write the letter. Set it out as you were advised in the previous exercise. Remember that if you write to a particular person you should end the letter *Yours sincerely*; use *Yours faithfully* if the letter begins *Dear Sir/Madam*.

NOTES

1 Always include details of previous experience and education. Emphasise details that you think will be relevant to the particular job.
2 *CV* means Curriculum Vitae – the details of your career. Names and addresses of referees, if they are asked for, should be written at the bottom of the letter either immediately before, or below, your signature.

A reference is a letter from someone who knows you (your Headmaster, for instance) that you will send with your application.

A referee is a person whom the employer will contact to ask about you. (Most employers prefer to use referees; they will probably give a fairer picture of you if they know you are not going to see the letter.)

Writing 2

Imagine the job you have chosen asks for a referee. Write to your Head, asking him or her to be a referee. The tone of the letter is important. For instance, which of these phrases might be sensible to use and which would not?

I bet you don't remember me
Please give my regards to Mr . . .
I suppose it shook you when I passed . . .
My form-teacher in my last year was Mrs . . .

Tell him or her the relevant details about the job and mention any previous jobs you have had since leaving school.

Writing 3

Imagine you have applied for the GARDENER GRADE IV job. This is the application form and job description you have been sent.

Complete the form and refer to the job description in the letter of application section.

ST LUKES HOSPITAL

Job Description

Gardener Grade IV

The person appointed will be under the general supervision of the Registrar, and will be responsible, with one junior assistant, for the maintenance of the gardens of the main hospital and those of the staff living quarters, one mile from the main site.

There is considerable scope for initiative and landscaping, as the gardens are large and some areas in need of re-organisation. There is a generous budget for the upkeep of the gardens, since they are regarded as an important factor in the patients' well-being, and the person appointed will be responsible for the management of the budget, both in the buying of equipment, seeds and plants, and the selling of produce - there is a small vegetable garden.

The person appointed will have previous experience and some horticultural qualification.

MIDSHIRE LOCAL AUTHORITY   Please complete this form in BLACK ink.

APPLICATION FOR POST OF GARDENER GRADE IV	Mr Ms Mrs Miss
1.(a) Name in full (surname first)	(a)
(b) (i) Permanent address and telephone number	(b) (i)
(ii) Address to which correspondence should be sent (if different from above) and telephone number	(ii)

Age	Date of Birth	Married or Single (a married woman or widow should give maiden name)

2. EDUCATION Schools from the age of 11 (give dates)		From	To

Have you any qualifications or interests which are relevant to this application?

Names and addresses of two persons from whom confidential references may be obtained.

Name	Address	Position
1.		
2.		

LETTER OF APPLICATION MUST BE IN OWN HANDWRITING

PARTICULARS OF PREVIOUS EXPERIENCE

From	To	Employer	Post held

If appointed, when could you begin duty?	If you are a registered disabled person please give registration number

I hereby certify that the entries on this form are complete and correct to the best of my knowledge.

Date....................   Signed.............................

Oral work 1

Work in pairs. Choose a job that asks for a telephone application. Tell your partner the job you intend to apply for. Make notes (without consulting each other) firstly of the details you will tell your partner, as the employer, on the telephone and secondly of the questions you will ask your partner when you become the employer and your partner rings you as an applicant.

    Now telephone each other, taking turns to be employer and applicant.

NOTE

It is more effective if you mime holding the telephone and do not look at each other during your conversation.

Oral work 2 – interviews

Imagine you have been called for interview for the job you applied for by letter (page 204).

In groups of four, take turns to be interviewers and applicant – three interviewers, one applicant.

You will need to prepare for the interviews by:

1 Looking at the advertisements for the jobs the other three members of your group have applied for.
2 Looking at the other letters of application.
3 Making notes on both advertisements and applications in preparation for your role as interviewer.

Take turns to be the chairperson of the interviewing panel. He or she will be in charge of the conduct of the interview, introducing the others to the candidate, and deciding the order of questioning.

NOTE

'Interview' implies two-way questioning – ask the candidate if he or she has questions for the panel.

▭▭◫▷ *LANGUAGE PRACTICE*

Appropriate language

Read this piece from *What the Butler Winked At*, by Eric Home, his life-history and his only book, written in 1923. At the beginning of the book the publishers have written:

> The Publishers considered putting this biography into more conventional form, but eventually decided to print it in the exact form it was received from the author.

Decide what the publishers meant by 'conventional form'. Put the piece in conventional form. Why did they eventually decide not to alter it? Do you think they were right?

What the Butler Winked At

1 Another thing you wont see is a crosseyed servant. They are as scarse as dead donkeys. These noble Lords can be crosseyed one-legged and Blind as Bats. Oh yes they are all right. They have got Blue Blood in their vanes. But their servants have to be perfect no smelly feet stinking under their Noble Noses.

5 There was this old titled lady. In Eaton Place she was. Very prowd of her matching footmen. When she was hireing them they had to walk backwards and forewards. Just so this old gel could watch their action. Like she was buying a horse. All their bits had to be well greased and in working order, you can bet. No, a servant cant be knock-kneed flat-footed, humpty-backed,

10 idiotic. The noble lords can be that and they usaully are. They like them well-thatched as well. Many a servant has lost his position if his thatch starts to fall off, I can tell you.

Eric Home

209

⬛⬛⬛▷ *EXAMINATION PRACTICE*

Read the quotations below from four people connected with Campston Youth
Custody Centre which takes young offenders aged between 16 and 21.
Use the quotations as a basis for your answer to *one* of the questions which
follow. You may add extra detail. Your writing should take about 25 lines.
Write appropriately and organise your material carefully.

Governor
This is an open centre . . . we take young offenders for sentences between six
months and a year . . . co-operation is rewarded by remission of one third of
the sentence . . . we refer to our offenders as trainees and indeed we make
every effort to teach them useful skills . . . we have few absconders.

Volunteer
(a person from outside who inspects conditions, talks to inmates and makes
reports to local authorities)
Although it is disappointing that 70 per cent of the inmates are convicted of
new offences within two years of release, I still feel that the centre, with its
accent on training, has a better chance of success than a prison atmosphere
where inmates are kept in cells for most of the day . . . the trainees I talk to are
usually anxious to co-operate and seem to take advantage of the educational
and training facilities . . . though of course they are keen to be released.

Trainee 1
The training they talk about is rubbish . . . there are a few places on car
maintenance and working in the boiler room isn't bad . . . at least it's warm . . .
but most of us end up slaving on the farm, picking stones, mending fences,
even milking cows . . . when I get back to London I'm sure to get a good job
milking cows! The screws thieve most of the farm produce . . . we're really
working for them.

Trainee 2
It's better than being in Wormwood Scrubs . . . I give you that . . . but it's not
going to reform anybody . . . if you go round 'sirring' the screws and
generally creeping you can be out of this place in five months . . . it's not much
of a deterrent . . . still, don't think I'm complaining . . . actually, if I'm honest
(and I am sometimes) I don't think it's a bad place . . . it's given me a bit of time
to think things out . . . and I'm going straight when I'm released . . . I'll give it a
try anyway.

Directed writing

Write *one* of the following.

1 A letter to the *Campston Gazette* from a volunteer visitor who feels that Campston Youth Custody Centre is not sufficient deterrent for young criminals and who favours a more traditional prison system.
2 A record of the discussion between the volunteer visitor above and the one quoted on the subject of the best method of treatment for young criminals. Invent names for the two visitors.
3 A letter from a trainee to his parents about his first impressions of Campston Youth Custody Centre.
4 A letter from the Governor replying to a newspaper criticism that if 70 per cent of the offenders commit new crimes within two years of release the system must be at fault.

Continuous writing

Choose *one* of the following. You may make up the material or use your own experiences. Be careful to check that you have written in paragraphs and that your full stops and spellings are correct.

A family reunion

1 Write about an occasion when one or more of your relatives were reunited with you after a long time. Describe your feelings before, during and immediately after the reunion.

2 **The pleasures and perils of being a collector**
   Do not limit yourself to describing your own experiences. Spend at least one paragraph making some comment on collectors in general, even those whose particular hobby seems to you odd or silly.

3 **Meeting new people**
   'I hate my first meeting with someone. You usually talk the most stupid, boring rubbish, just for something to say.'

   Write two conversations between yourself and a stranger. In one write the type of conversation you usually have; in the second write the conversation you would like to have.

Continuous writing

Further titles and suggestions

You are asked to write clearly and effectively, to spell and punctuate correctly, and to ensure that your writing is appropriate in style and content to the subject chosen.

Write about 300–400 words.

Before you write your full answers, make a short plan.

1 **'I must get rid of it.'**
Write a story either beginning or ending with these words.

2 The Ideal Home Exhibition offers a competition for the design of a kitchen or workroom.
Without the aid of diagrams write an entry for the competition describing the layout and the equipment.

3 Write a set of instructions for somebody who is looking after your house while you are on holiday. You may need to invent pets, plants and other factors that will need attention.
Write 100–150 words, setting out your instructions in the clearest possible manner.

4 **Monday morning**
Write in any way you wish, but if you choose to recount your typical Monday morning include the feelings you associate with both the beginning of the week and your Monday morning activities.

5 During your holidays you are asked to make a selection of books for a younger brother or sister, or a young visitor. Describe your choices and say how you would set about persuading the younger persons to read them.

6 **'I soon realised I had made a mistake.'**
Write a story beginning with these words.

7   'You look as if you wished the place in Hell,'
   My friend said, 'judging by your face.' 'Oh well,
   I suppose it's not the place's fault,' I said.
These lines are from a Philip Larkin poem about the town in which he spent his childhood.
What are your views about your town or village? Include some incidents in your life that were directly connected with your surroundings.

8 Write about 250 words on one of the pictures opposite. You may write a story, a description or a newspaper report. There must be a clear connection between your writing and the picture.

9 Write a report, suitable for a newspaper or magazine, in which you give your impression of a recent holiday. Include comments on the price, the facilities, the ease or difficulty of the organisation and the suitability for various age groups.

10 Write an estate agent's advertisement for your own house. Include details such as the number of rooms, their size, and convenience for shops and buses.

11 **'A journey I'll never forget.'**

The journey may be interesting, frightening, beautiful or nightmarish. Compare your feelings at the beginning and the end of the journey.

12 Write a story which illustrates one of the proverbs.
    Look before you leap.
    A fool and his money are soon parted.

13 **Unwelcome visitors**

You may tell a story, make general comments and illustrate from your experience, or write advising how to cope with the problem.

14 **A conversation piece**

Write in the form of a play, a conversation between two people whose views are radically opposed. Allow the conversation to develop (there may be more than one subject).

15 You receive an invitation to stay with a friend. You would like to go but unfortunately you have already promised to visit a relation during the same week. Make a decision and write a letter to the friend and the relative.

16 Design a poster advertisement for a food or a household gadget. Use more than one colour if you wish but concentrate on the design and wording.

17 **The power of television**

Write about the power of television to influence people's lives. You may write generally or give an account of how you have been powerfully influenced.

18 **'That was the last I saw of him (or her).'**

Write a story ending with these words.

19 Imagine you have suddenly become famous (or infamous). Write, as if you were a newspaper reporter, an article about your sudden rise to fame.

20 Write about a fight, successful or unsuccessful, against overwhelming odds.

Skills reference section

A mistake in spelling, punctuation or grammar is called 'careless' if the writer can find the error for himself when asked to look at a particular word or sentence.

'Careless' is often unfair; the writer does care, but there are so many aspects of writing to worry about that accuracy often suffers, especially when struggling with what to say, how to organise the material, and with the expressions best suited to the purpose.

Good habits

Use this section to check your particular weaknesses after each piece of writing. You might be prone to mis-spelling certain words, using commas instead of full stops, omitting or mis-using apostrophes, missing out question marks, mis-using speech marks or even using particular clumsy phrases.

You will probably not learn anything new in this section, but if you check your weaknesses and use the practice exercises you will be cultivating good habits, and making appropriate usage automatic, so that you can concentrate on the important parts of writing – what you say and how you say it.

▷ Direct speech

Direct speech enlivens writing but it is the biggest source of error for most pupils. These five lines contain most of the mistakes you can make. Check that you know the error at each point underlined.

> 'Where are you going,' asked Bill_
> 'thats none of your business.' I told him.
> 'It is if you're going to borrow my bike._
> 'I won't hurt it, you lend it to Bill.'
> 'Get your hands off that bike!!' 'Else what?'

NOTE

Errors such as omitting apostrophes and using a comma where a full stop is needed are more common in direct speech, even though they are not actual speech mark errors.

Skills reference section

Practice

Develop a conversation of ten lines from one of these. Concentrate only on accuracy; do not worry about developing an interesting conversation.

a) 'Why are you hiding round this corner?' asked the caretaker.
b) 'You're late again,' said John.
c) 'I bet you sent that horrible valentine card,' said Jane.

Ask someone to mark your work, making a separate check for each of the mistakes in the five lines on page 215.

Read this dialogue

'I bet you sent that horrible valentine card,' said Jane.
'There was nothing horrible about it. Don't you like roses?' said Andrew.
'Oh, you sent me that one, did you? I'm sorry. I thought you sent the hippo one.'
'What hippo?'
'It was a hippo in red knickers. Supposed to be me.'
'A hippo in red knickers. Are you sure?'
'Of course, I'm sure. Why?'
'Did you get any other animal cards? I mean like an elephant or something.'
'You mean like an elephant in a yellow bikini? Caught you, thicko. You sent two cards. The nice one to put me off the scent.'
'Yes, but what about the hippo one?'
'There wasn't one, idiot. I made it up to trick you into admitting the elephant. Now run for your miserable life!'

Write a piece of dialogue where there is some development, such as this. For instance, try to give the person hiding round the corner a convincing answer to all the caretaker's questions. (Practice (a), above.)

Ask someone to check your piece of dialogue. It is much more difficult to be accurate when you are thinking carefully what to say. It is even more difficult when you are writing a longer piece in a limited time.

Practise dialogue on your own at regular intervals. If you concentrate on developing conversations in a set time then you will be reproducing the conditions of a timed longer piece.

Keep practising and checking to achieve the good habit of accurate conversation.

 ▷ **Apostrophes**

A separate check of each piece of work for apostrophe mistakes will eventually get you in the habit of looking while you are writing.

Omission

The apostrophe which takes the place of letters omitted when words are run together (*hadn't, couldn't*) is easy to place correctly. Anyone who writes *did'nt* is certainly being careless.
The problem is remembering to put them in.

Practice

Write out the words you generally use that need an apostrophe to show letters have been omitted. You will then see the size of the problem. There aren't so many and they are probably all connected with the verbs *to be, to have* and *to do.*

   Make yourself re-write the list every time you make this type of mistake in your writing. Eventually you will develop an automatic signal when you write the words.

NOTE

six 'o'clock is a common error for *six o'clock.* It is short for 'six of the clock' and only one apostrophe is needed – where the four letters have been omitted.

Possession

This apostrophe is one of the two most common sources of mistakes in English. (The other is using a comma where a stronger stop is needed – see page 215.) The rules often confuse people. If you have difficulty refer to these practical hints.

1 Do not use apostrophes on the pronouns:

yours   hers   ours   theirs   its

you would not think of using an apostrophe on *mine* or *his*, which are the same type of pronoun.

NOTE

It's is short for it is or it has and must be distinguished from 'its tail'.

2 Learn these four words where the apostrophe will always be in the same place:

women's   men's   children's   people's

3 Add examples to this list:

that girl's school   —   a girls' school
a year's work   —   in two years' time

It is sometimes better to learn the rules by deducing them yourself from a series of examples.

4 Learn these:

barber's   grocer's   hairdresser's

Add four more.

Notice that the apostrophe is still needed even when the word that makes it necessary – shop – has been omitted.

▷ Full stops

Read this piece by a fourth-year pupil.

> 'It was a cold October morning fog swirled round the station, the birds were still, it was too cold to sing. A train arrived and broke the silence, this seemed to signal the start of the day, I entered my carriage and sat next to a dirty window, I looked out filth and dirt seemed to have taken over the whole station.'

If the writer were told that he had not divided the piece correctly into sentences, he would probably make two or three alterations. If he were told there were six places where he should have started a new sentence, he would almost certainly find all six and be able to correct them.

You should develop the good habit of checking the accuracy of your sentences without needing to be prompted.

You can develop this habit by working on the sentence structure of your own or others' writing.

Practice

1 Write out the passage on the previous page, using nine sentences.
2 Write it in four sentences using five conjunctions, each linking two or three sentences into one.

FOR EXAMPLE:

'The birds were still *because* it was too cold to sing.'

> NOTE

Frequent reference to this list of common conjunctions will help you improve the variety of your sentence structure and check its accuracy.

and but when where because as though although
since that so what if

> NOTE

Then is *not* a conjunction.

3 Sentences can also be linked by replacing one of the main verbs with the *ing* form of the verb – a participle.

FOR EXAMPLE:

'Seizing his chance, he leapt over the barrier.'

Link these pairs of sentences by replacing one verb with a participle.

a) The train arrived. The train broke the silence.
b) She knew the answer to question three. She wrote it down immediately.
c) James spotted the rare bird. He carefully raised his camera.

▷ Watch your sentences

The best way of ensuring that your sentences are grammatically correct is to understand the variety of effects that can be achieved by varying the length and structure of your sentences.

A series of short sentences is often appropriate for

a) explanation, particularly of a difficult process. The reader is given time to digest the information.
b) an exciting part of a story. The staccato effect reflects the tension.

Longer sentences are often appropriate for

a) descriptive passages. The details of the description will make a better impact if they are accumulated together in longer sentences.
b) passages where a climax is being built. Often a short sentence as a climax to a series of longer ones will increase the effect.

Skills reference section

Read these beginnings of three famous novels. Punctuate them in the way you think most suitable with commas and full stops. Use the library to check your punctuation with the original.

We are at rest five miles behind the front yesterday we were relieved and now our bellies are full of beef and haricot beans we are satisfied and at peace each man has another mess tin full for the evening and what is more there is a double ration of sausage and bread that puts a man in fine trim

All Quiet on the Western Front, Erich Maria Remarque

Mr Jones of the Manor Farm had locked the hen-house for the night but was too drunk to remember to shut the pop-holes with the ring of light from his lantern dancing from side to side he lurched across the yard kicking off his boots at the back door drew himself a last glass of beer from the barrel in the scullery and made his way up to bed where Mrs Jones was already snoring

Animal Farm, George Orwell

If you really want to hear about it the first thing you'll probably want to know is where I was born and what my lousy childhood was like and how my parents were occupied and all before they had me and all that David Copperfield kind of crap but I don't feel like going into it in the first place that stuff bores me and in the second place my parents would have about two haemorrhages apiece if I told anything pretty personal about them they're quite touchy about anything like that especially my father

The Catcher in the Rye, J D Salinger

Dickens fails GCSE

Punctuate this passage from the beginning of *A Tale of Two Cities* by Charles Dickens. When you look up the original you will discover that he has lost enough marks in his first paragraph to fail at GCSE.

It was the best of times it was the worst of times it was the age of wisdom it was the age of foolishness it was the epoch of belief it was the season of Light it was the spring of hope it was the winter of despair we had everything before us we had nothing before us we were all going direct to heaven we were all going direct the other way.

This passage shows that there are no unalterable rules of writing. But you need to know them well before you break them.

Compare your version with the original. Why has Dickens decided to use commas instead of full stops?

▷ Spelling

Only the most inaccurate pieces of writing have more than twenty spelling errors in a composition of five hundred words – that is 4 per cent of the words used.

People know how to spell almost all the words they commonly use; they simply keep mis-spelling the same ones, because they fail to look them up or ask when they feel they might be wrong.

Use this list of the hundred most commonly mis-spelt words as a miniature dictionary. Add to the list any other words that you spell incorrectly.

accommodation	disappear	parallel
accurate	disappoint	parliament
achieve	disapprove	pavilion
across	eager	persuade
address	embarrassment	physical
advertisement	erected	possess
agreeable	especially	practice (n)/practise (v)
amount	exaggerate	preferred
appearance	exercise	privilege
appointment	favourite	professional
argument	finally	queue
beautiful	foreign	quite (adv)/quiet (adj)
beginning	fortunately	receive
behaviour	guard	relief
believe	height	reminisced
business	humorous	responsible
cautious	imaginary	restaurant
centre	immediately	ridiculous
character	impatiently	scarcely
cheque/check	impressive	separate
cigarette	ladies	shoulder
coarse (adj)/course (n)	loneliness	seize
colour	lose (v)/loose (adj)	similar
committee	machinery	sincerely
competition	minute	soldier
conscious	necessary	stepped
criticise/criticize	neighbour	straight
deceive	neither	strangely
definitely	nuisance	success
descend	occasional	surprise
description	occurred	tragedy
development	opportunity	until
different	opposite	vicious
		vigorous

Beware – grammar traps in operation

Acceptable English changes with usage. For instance in an old poem *The Jackdaw of Rheims*, the people were so excited by the discovery of the Jackdaw thefts

> 'That heedless of grammar, they all cried "That's him".'

That's he would sound very formal nowadays. Usage of *that's him* has made it acceptable.

There are, nevertheless, still many traps to avoid. Each of these sentences contains a point of grammar, style or word choice which in careful writing you should try to avoid. They could cause confusion or misunderstanding on the part of the reader, even though some of them could be used appropriately in speech. See if you can identify the problem in these sentences.

1 Jane literally flew down the track in her new spikes.
2 The car was in front of the house, not the bus.
3 Nobody dared say what they really thought.
4 Both girls were tall, but Joan was the tallest.
5 I was surprised to meet Jack whom I thought was in America.
6 Share it between Julie and I.
7 I felt sorry for him, lying in hospital.
8 I'm looking for a chair for an old lady with a wide seat, long back and short legs.
9 There are less pupils in school this year.
10 A list of all the people present, and their countries of origin, were put in the hotel foyer.

> NOTE

These points will help you to work out the answers.

a) *literally* is the opposite of metaphorically. It means 'in the exact sense of the word – without metaphor'

b) *misunderstandings* (ambiguities) will arise if a phrase is wrongly placed in a sentence (nos. 2, 7 and 8)

c) *Nobody, anybody, everybody, each* and *every* are singular – they refer to many people but do so one at a time. So they must have singular verbs and other parts of speech.

FOR EXAMPLE:
Each of the parents *was* allowed to give *his* or *her* opinion.

d) *Comparative/Superlative*
Comparative (*taller, older, abler*) for two.
Superlative (*tallest, oldest, ablest*) for more than two.

e) *Pronouns*
If the subject of a verb: *I, he, she, we, they*
If the object of a verb or after a preposition: *me, him, us, them*
   So 'between you and *me*'.

f) *who/whom* — *who* if subject of verb
                — *whom* if object or after a preposition

FOR EXAMPLE
He saw the man *whom* he hated (object of *hated*)
He saw the man *who* hated him (subject of *hated*)
There's the girl for *whom* he waited all his life (*whom* because after preposition 'for')

g) *less* does not mean *not so many*

h) Agreement of verbs with subjects – singular subject, singular verb.

FOR EXAMPLE:
A *list* of people *is* . . .
Lists of people *are* . . .

Index